2/97

IN THEIR OWN WORDS

A PIONEER WOMAN'S MEMOIR

IN THEIR OWN WORDS

A PIONEER WOMAN'S MEMOIR

Based on the Journal of Arabella Clemens Fulton

Judith E. Greenberg and Helen Carey McKeever

FRANKLIN WATTS
New York / Chicago / London / Toronto / Sydney

This is the first book in a series entitled "In Their Own Words." Each book presents the writings of a person who lived during a significant time period or event in America's history. The records of the writers' thoughts, experiences, and feelings have been preserved and are, in this series, offered to today's readers.

Photographs copyright ©: Oregon Historical Society: pp. 12 (0RHI5231), 20 (0RHI83930), 58 (0RHI23551), 131 (ORHI791), 151 (CN#006109); Stock Montage: pp. 16, 29, 66, 84, 109; New York Public Library, Picture Collection: p. 25; The Bettmann Archive: pp. 35, 40, 49, 75, 104, 141; The National Archives: pp. 62, 124, 136, 144; North Wind Picture Archives: pp. 70, 79, 89, 92, 95, 99, 117, 147.

Library of Congress Cataloging-in-Publication Data

Fulton, Arabella, 1844–1934
     [Memoir. Selections]
     A pioneer woman's memoir / by Judith E. Greenberg and Helen Carey McKeever.
          p. cm. — (In their own words)
     Includes index.
     ISBN 0-531-11211-X (lib. bdg.)
     1. Fulton, Arabella, 1844–1934. 2. West (U.S.) — Description and travel. 3. West (U.S.) — History — 1860–1890. 4. Pioneers — West (U.S.) — Biography. 5. Women pioneers — West (U.S.) — Biography. [1. Fulton, Arabella, 1844–1934. 2. Pioneers. 3. Women — Biography. 4. Overland journeys to the Pacific. 5. Oregon Trail. 6. West (U.S.) — History.] I. Greenberg, Judith E. II. McKeever, Helen Carey. III. Title. IV. Series.
F594.F8   1995
978'.02'092—dc20
[B]   94-48043
                                             CIP AC

ACKNOWLEDGMENTS

We would like to thank the many descendants of Arabella Clemens Fulton for their generosity in sharing the memoir of their grandmother with the reader. These relatives, like Arabella herself, saw the value of making her memoir available to young people who could learn so much from the words of a true pioneer. The grandchildren with whom we spoke and corresponded were most kind and gave freely of their time to tell us anecdotes and family history, which helped to make Arabella even more real to us, and even more interesting.

We would also like to thank Jean Borteck and Mary Ann Breskin for their help in finding the memoir of Arabella Clemens Fulton.

To Sharon Hellman and Patty Goldberg
J.E.G.

*To a special friend, Laurabelle Gaitens, of
McDonald, Pennsylvania*
H.C.M.

CONTENTS

MEETING ARABELLA

From my observation I think the womenfolk on these long travels did more than double duty in caring for the children, preparing the food, and bearing the brunt of irritated tempers. In fact, I think woman might well claim the credit for settling and civilizing the great Northwest, for without her help it never would have been settled. She encouraged the undertaking, shared all the hardships, faced dangers and privations with fortitude and resolution, and was, indeed, "a helpmeet" in upbuilding this Northwest Empire.
     — Arabella Clemens Fulton

ARABELLA CLEMENS FULTON, the writer of this memoir, set out for the West in April 1864. She was one of an estimated 300,000 to 350,000 men, women, and children who, in 75,000 wagons, traveled over at least part of the Oregon Trail in the early 1840s to the late 1860s, seeking cheap land on the Great Plains and in Oregon Territory.

She took part in one of the greatest peacetime migrations in all history—one that consumed the longest time and covered the greatest distance—accomplished by men and women wanting a better life.

Arabella, like most of the other women who helped to settle the West, experienced great emotional, physical, mental, and social changes as she confronted an unknown world far from her original home. By writing her memoir,

An evening camp along the Oregon Trail

Arabella hoped to leave a record for her children and their children "of our migration to the West, and of our life there, my own experiences being typical of others' in upbuilding the great West."

Arabella Fulton's memoir is private writing, with the unguarded intimacy that creates compelling reading. However, reading a memoir or a diary requires a bit of work because neither can be read as an ordinary story can be. In an ordinary story there is a beginning, a middle, and an end. But in a memoir or diary the thoughts are more random and spontaneous. The writer may move from topic to topic within a sentence or paragraph, and months and years can go by with little or no mention of a topic.

Another important point to remember is that in private

writings, an author may reveal attitudes, ideas, and misconceptions that might be covered over or modified in more formal writing. In this memoir, Arabella shows herself to be a young Southern woman, loyal to her family, her society, and the only way of life she has known. Caught up in the emotions of the Civil War period, she speaks frankly of her resentment of "over-zealous" Northern sympathizers, of their cruel behavior toward slaveholders, and their lack of respect for property rights. She displays little understanding of other issues at the heart of the slavery debate: human rights and the moral problems inherent in the institution of slavery. In writing about her experiences while meeting Indians, she again echoes her society, revealing ignorance of the Indian civilizations and paying little attention to the fact that the settlers were appropriating lands where the Indians had lived for centuries. In editing Arabella's memoir, we thought about omitting some of this material. However, our purpose is not to change or sanitize history, but to allow readers to experience it more directly. Arabella's writings reflect her own personality as well as the ideas and sentiments of her society in her time. Perhaps another purpose of this book is to allow us an opportunity to appraise what we have learned in the decades since Arabella compiled her record.

Arabella Clemens Fulton's original memoir contains nearly 400 pages. We have kept the original organization of Arabella's memoir. That is, we use chapters as she did, but we have broken the narrative into fewer chapters and shortened many of them. We have deleted repetitious details about people and events, and eliminated some minor incidents and entries that do not provide important information or add to the reader's understanding of Arabella's world. Also, but only when necessary, we have modernized some nineteenth-century spellings and inserted modern place names in place of those no longer in use.

Woven through the memoir are the threads of five major themes that stand out boldly. These are: Arabella's admiration of courage, her belief in treating other human beings with decency and kindness, her faith in the economic opportunities offered by the West, her conviction that hard work is the way to achieve goals, and her certainty of the importance of family. Throughout her memoir, Arabella's gentle and pleasant voice makes clear her feelings about the great national adventure in which she took part.

Through her memoir we are able to watch Arabella, young and inexperienced at the beginning of the journey, become transformed by the challenges she faces into a strong woman, a caring mother, a dutiful and loving wife, and a helpful neighbor. A woman emerges who is determined that her family will survive and even thrive despite danger, isolation, exhaustion, illness, and intense deprivation. And because of what we learn from her experiences, we are able to develop a glimmering of understanding of what all people must feel when they leave the places and people they know and are confronted by rapid change and the unknown. Also, through her story of her participation in the "great adventure," we can better understand the impact of the pioneer experience on the emigrants' lives, changing them and the nation forever. Finally, we learn about hope and its persistence in the midst of mistakes and failures. It is for all of these reasons and more that we feel Arabella Clemens Fulton's memoir is remarkable.

When we first meet her, Arabella is young Arabella Clemens, a lively, adventurous twenty-year-old who decides to go to live in the West with her two sisters and their husbands. Remaining in Missouri are her father and several younger brothers and sisters. More than six decades later, when she is in her eighties, Arabella Clemens Fulton, at the urging of her children, begins putting down on paper her memories of the hardships, dangers, dreams, and accomplishments of the pioneers who, like herself, traveled the Oregon Trail and settled the American West.

This is her story. And, in a very real way, it is yours, too.

14

1

MOVING WEST

I have lived in the West since the year 1864. At that time it was a country in the wilds, inhabited by savage Indians, with just a sprinkling of white trappers and gold hunters whose appearance hardly distinguished them from savages. But they were good-hearted and hospitable withal. I have watched the great change and improvement in the country with wonder and amazement.

OVER 150 YEARS AGO the first major wagon train traveled west on the 2,000-mile Oregon Trail. The pioneers who joined the wagon trains came from the East, the South, and from Europe, hoping to establish new homes in the West. The American frontier, with its many thousands of acres of open land, held a powerful attraction for ambitious homesteaders.

The Oregon Territory was particularly appealing. At the beginning of the 1840s fewer than 500 Americans were living in the Oregon country. Then the Willamette River Valley caught the nation's attention when missionaries and other early visitors to Oregon issued glowing reports of the region and its cheap, rich land and gentle climate.

The government made establishing new homes in the West easier for the pioneers by passing the Homestead Act of 1862. This act offered 160 acres free to a person who would settle and make improvements on this land. Any adult citizen or adult person declaring an intention to become a citizen was eligible. With all these inducements, it was small wonder that thousands of peo-

15

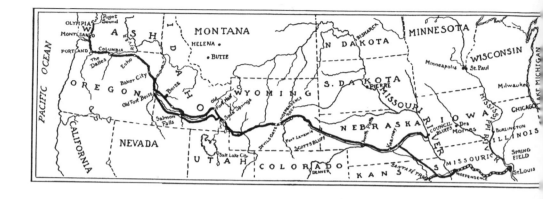

The Oregon Trail

ple in Europe and America began to pull up stakes and head for Oregon.

Among those who caught "Oregon fever" and decided to move west were Arabella Clemens, her two sisters and their husbands, who sought not only a fresh start in the new land, but also an opportunity to leave the chaos of the Civil War behind them.

M y people were of the South. My father came from Tennessee, his father from Kentucky; my mother was also from Kentucky. They were of that migration crossing the Cumberlands under the leadership of Daniel Boone, settling in the valleys of Kentucky and Tennessee. Later, again influenced by the glowing reports of Boone, they came to Boone County, Missouri, forming a great settlement of friends and kindred.

Though he was from Tennessee and she from Kentucky, my father and mother met in Boone

County, where they had grown to young manhood and womanhood, and were married.

I was three years old when they moved up to Linn County, in order to get larger land holdings. Here we met the gallant and scholarly Colonel Flournoy, a gentleman of the Old South, wealthy in lands and slaves. Our acquaintance soon ripened into a warm, intimate friendship, which lasted for many years.

I recall a visit to my maternal grandmother, Jesse Turner, in Boone County, after I had become pretty much of a young lady. My Grandfather Turner was a man of influence in the state, and was one of the founders of the University of Columbia, now the state-supported University of Missouri. He was also prominent in political affairs, and had something to do in shaping governmental matters in his county and state.

We were on the frontier of a pioneer country. Living was hard, schooling meager, and times were unsettled. The slavery question was a burning issue, and the mutterings of War ever in the air. But we worked and strove to open up the farm and make living conditions better. Let it be understood that the children of slave owners were not always exempt from hard labor. The story of the early settlers of the middle states is a matter of history, to which I could add nothing, and further, is divergent from the purpose of this writing. I propose to write of our migration to the West, and of our life there, my own experiences being typical of others' in upbuilding the great West.

The story of the border states of Missouri and Kansas is well-known, and of the bitterness and crime engendered in the struggle for supremacy between the slavery and the anti-slavery forces much has been written. It is not for me to recount them here. We lived in that part of the state where the James boys, driven to desperation by the outrages of the War, began their course of outlawry, seeking to avenge their wrongs. When the War began, guerrilla warfare soon spread over our section, gripping it in a reign of terror.

I was born in 1844, and I lived on the border until the last year of the Civil War. My father, John W. Clemens, was a slave owner and during this period, before the Emancipation Proclamation, all slave owners here were looked upon with suspicion by the government agents, and soon became targets for the petty spites and indignities of over-zealous partisans favoring the North. In many instances slave owners and suspected Southern sympathizers were accorded atrocious treatment, in some cases the treatment extended to murder.

My father, a strong admirer of Henry Clay, "the Great Compromiser," was never in sympathy with the extremists of the South. I heard him say, at the time South Carolina seceded, that "she needed a right good thrashing," and "she should have waited to see what methods Lincoln would adopt." But when Missouri was put under military rule—largely through the hot-headedness of General Lyon, who was later killed in the Battle of Wilson Creek, he, together with others of the most substantial citizenry of the community, was arrested, taken to military headquarters, and there made to take the oath of allegiance to his country, when, in fact, none of them had ever been disloyal, either in thought or in deed. He considered such treatment an uncalled-for indignity, and one hard to bear.

When the War broke out soon there sprung up over the whole state self-appointed "patriotic" organizations, having for their purpose coercion and intimidation of the people, and the members of these organizations, under the names of Home Leaguers and Home Guards, perpetrated all sorts of cruelty, and outraged the rights of the citizens.

As time went on, these abuses became so cruel that nobody was safe in life or property, and the people of our neighborhood became so utterly discouraged and disgusted as the War progressed, that finally they reached the point where they began to discuss the possibility of making up a wagon train and moving to Oregon.

Such a venture as this, however, would be no small undertaking, and to equip for it would require much money, which at that time was a scarce article in our community. Those going would first have to dispose of their property, which would bring only a pittance, while the supplies and equipment required for the journey would be very costly. In other words, we would have to sell low and buy high—a ruinous move at the beginning. But there seemed to be no other way out of the difficulty.

Other momentous problems also had to be met before the expedition could get under way. Farms had to be sold and personal property disposed of; wagons, teams, and supplies for the journey had to be obtained; release from military service was necessary for many of those eligible for the draft. Paroled Confederate soldiers had to obtain permits to leave the state, and there were many other requirements to be met.

The more the venture was talked about, agitated, and prepared for, the stronger the excitement grew until it spread from neighborhood to neighborhood, from vicinity to vicinity, and before we realized it, the fervor had assumed large proportions. Inquiries came from remote districts seeking information relative to the proposed expedition. Soon meetings were being called in the various communities, and advisory boards were being appointed with a view to organizing the train.

All winter interest in the undertaking ran high, and as spring drew near, the promoters in our vicin-

19

A

GENERAL CIRCULAR

TO ALL

PERSONS OF GOOD CHARACTER,

WHO WISH TO EMIGRATE

TO THE

OREGON TERRITORY,

EMBRACING SOME ACCOUNT OF THE CHARACTER AND
ADVANTAGES OF THE COUNTRY ; THE RIGHT
AND THE MEANS AND OPERATIONS BY
WHICH IT IS TO BE SETTLED;—

AND

ALL NECESSARY DIRECTIONS FOR BECOMING

AN EMIGRANT.

Hall J. Kelley, *General Agent.*

BY ORDER OF THE AMERICAN SOCIETY FOR ENCOURAGING

the SETTLEMENT of the OREGON TERRITORY.

INSTITUTED IN BOSTON, A.D. 1829.

CHARLESTOWN:
PRINTED BY WILLIAM W. WHEILDON.
R. P. & C. WILLIAMS—BOSTON.
1831.

A *"General Circular"* of 1831 encouraged
prospective emigrants to join the movement
west, following the Oregon Trail.

ity thought it advisable to call a meeting of all our neighbors who contemplated making the journey, to make definite arrangements and to determine how many wagons they would take in the train. The meeting was largely attended; it was learned that many more people were trying to get ready than had at first been expected. Harmony and good will prevailed, and all expressed the desire to help each other as much as they could in disposing of property and making arrangements for the journey.

Now, since they had definitely decided to undertake the venture and the time for preparation was short, everyone went to work quietly all winter disposing of their homes and belongings. Many who had been undecided, and fearful that they could not meet the undertaking, took new courage at the meeting and decided to go. There were many others, too, who wanted to go, but could not. How they longed for the opportunity, and planned for it, but could not accomplish it! My father was one of these. He had a good farm but he could not sell it. He had a family of small children dependent upon him. Plan as he might, there seemed no way for him to go.

But he had three daughters, caught in the whirlpool of the excitement, who did go. These were my twin sisters, Addie and Angie, two years younger than I, and myself. Both of the twins had married the previous year, and their husbands strongly desired to go. At first, my sisters sorely objected to going, for they imagined that all sorts of dangers beset the Trail, Indian massacres especially. However, after much persuasion they finally told their husbands they would go, providing I could go with them. I had been a sort of mother to them since the death of our mother a few years before, and they seemed to have confidence in my ability to take care of them.

There appeared to be no good reason why I should

not go. Surely I wanted to go! I was not particularly needed at home; my father had married again, and the smaller children now had a good stepmother. I could well be spared from household duties, so I willingly agreed to go with the twins if they could make room for me.

I was young then, just twenty, with all the romance and reality of life before me, eager for adventure, full of life and activity, and with no element of fear in my makeup. Then, too, I strongly resented the repressions I had to put upon my sympathies for the South. My people were of the South, and naturally, my sympathies were with them. But I dared not express my feelings in any way, for it would only bring more trouble on my father. I was glad now of the chance to get away from it all, and to seek new freedom in the open spaces of the West where my girlish utterances would not bring condemnation to my people.

2
TRAIL
PREPARATION

As the plans for the venture ripened and the people began to make preparations for the journey, they were confronted first of all by the food problem.

THE PIONEERS traveling the Oregon Trail hoped to reach their destination in four or five months. If all went well, the food that they packed In the wagons plus the fresh meat they expected to shoot would be sufficient to meet their needs.

Their plan was based on the hope that the prairie grass would be green and tall enough to feed the wagon train's livestock. A late start was to be avoided as the livestock of preceding wagon trains might have already consumed most of the grass along the Trail.

By the time that Arabella and her family were preparing to leave Missouri, there were guidebooks that recommended the items necessary for the long journey. Most guidebooks estimated that the cost for four people would be about $600.00, if they went on the Trail by wagon train with an ox team. A typical list of supplies and the suggested quantities appears on page 24.

With all the supplies packed inside and two people aboard, a covered wagon with iron rims on its wheels weighed nearly three thousand pounds.

FOOD AND FOOD PREPARATION	EQUIPMENT AND TOOLS	OTHER SUPPLIES
tin plates, cups, knives, and forks	4 yokes of oxen	candles
kettle, frypan, coffeepot	tent	soap
4 barrels of flour or cornmeal	wagon	matches
	wagon cover	quilts
50 lbs. of salt	45 lbs. of bedding	cotton & wool clothing
bacon	25 lbs. of gun-powder	medicines
lard	3 each of rifles and pistols	
50 lbs. of rice	30 lbs. of lead	
25 lbs. of molasses/ sugar	shovel, axe, hammer	
50 lbs. of coffee beans and tea		
dried fruits		
salaratus (baking soda)		
boxes of crackers and biscuits		

Such table supplies as sugar and coffee were not only high in price, but so exceedingly scarce that we could hardly get them at all. Flour too was high and scarce, cornmeal taking its place in our homes. But on a journey such as was now being contemplated, cornmeal was an undesirable substitute for flour, for its keeping qualities were not very satisfactory. However, some of the people who went in the train took cornmeal, and they said it proved to be better than they expected.

Meat could easily be procured, for at that time it was mainly all home-grown and home-cured, and was a staple article of diet in all households. Having no canned fruits in those days, we could take only dried apples and dried peaches. Rice was plentiful and we took a considerable quantity of it with us on the journey, but we had no milk or butter for seasoning it.

Eastern pioneers form a wagon train to head west.

Some took along butter packed in stone jars, but it didn't last long. We could easily meet the problem of wearing apparel, for our clothing was all home-made, and of homespun cloth of our own weaving. But being mostly woolen, it would be quite heavy and warm for summer wear. This necessitated the purchase of cotton goods for lighter clothing, which added considerably to the cost of outfitting ourselves, for cotton was scarce and costly.

It soon became evident that such a multitude of necessary items would be required for the trip, and money was so scarce and so hard to obtain outside of army employment, that there were many contemplating the journey who laid awake nights figuring how they could meet all these demands.

25

Although we had a little coffee in the train, parched wheat was used as a substitute, and each family took with them several sacks of wheat for this purpose, and had a little coffee-mill for grinding it. Many families took homemade syrup or sorghum, but these items were so heavy and bulky and took up so much room in the wagon train that not all were able to bring them.

We had no baking powders or soda for bread making, but used salaratus instead. It was much stronger than soda and had to be made into a liquid before using. Knowing that we would not be able to obtain fuel for baking along part of our way, we took along several boxes of crackers and sweet biscuit, both of which served a good purpose as a substitute for bread. A few potatoes also were taken, but their bulk made it impossible to take as many as we would need.

Our bill of fare on the journey was made up principally of fried fat meats and gravy made of water in which we sopped our bread. When we camped long enough we baked light bread, setting our cup of rising the night before, but this kind of bread making required a whole day's camping. Our unit, that is, those of our immediate family, were fortunate in having with us a sack of dark brown sugar, which we used for making syrup. There may have been others also who had sugar but I do not recall them. It was in this meager manner and with such staple articles that we met the food problem.

Now began the procuring of good wagons and suitable teams. Ox teams were the cheaper to outfit, for the cost of harness alone for horses was a considerable item. But many who already owned horses used them on the journey. It was necessary to take some grain to feed the stock at the beginning of the journey, for the grass was yet too young and tender to afford proper nourishment for the hard-worked teams, but it was expected that a few weeks later the prairie grass, said to grow abundantly along the Trail would be sufficient for their needs.

As the time for our departure drew nearer we were amazed at the widespread interest in the expedition, and at the number of people who were preparing to go. The "Oregon fever" had broken out in remote sections of the country, and we could expect a large emigration on the Oregon Trail this year. Our own train would be much larger than we had expected.

Judging from our own immediate neighborhood, the finances of the train would be very low—so low, indeed, that I now marvel how men could have had the courage to venture on so long and perilous a journey with so little money—going as they were into the unknown, unsettled, strange land where there was every reason to believe that they would meet with nothing but hard times.

One man with a wife and child told me that after he had his wagon and team all equipped and ready to start he had just seventy-five dollars left to pay for the expenses of the trip and a winter's living at the journey's end. Doubtless there were others better supplied than he, yet I do know that the finances of the train were exceedingly low, and that it required great faith and courage to undertake the venture. But behind it all was the thought of getting away from the hateful, blighting effects of the War. It could truthfully be said that the War brought the settlement of this great Northwest and Western country, and laid the foundation for the vast empire it has become. After the War was ended, the South, too, gave lavishly of her best blood to the West and Northwest. All who could possibly find a way to escape the sordid effects of the War did so. Out of the hideousness of the War was built this great Western domain.

3
GETTING UNDER WAY

Other trains were forming and rushing to get ahead of us, as though it were a race to see which would arrive first. But our captain kept a cool head and avoided confusion and hurry in our train.

THE PREFERRED JUMPING-OFF PLACE for wagon trains was Independence, Missouri, because it could be reached by steamboat on the Missouri River. The Santa Fe Trail started at this point as well. The town was well stocked with supplies and livestock available at reasonable prices for wagon trains preparing for the journey west. However, there were other, smaller freight suppliers and other starting points, and it was at one of these—Nebraska City—that Arabella's wagon train began its journey. Most of the wagon trains set out by the first week in May and moved at the rate of three miles an hour.

Huge herds of cows, calves, horses, mules, and oxen accompanied the covered wagons, raising great clouds of dust that tormented the travelers. The leader of a wagon train assigned positions for the wagons in the train but rotated them frequently so that no one wagon was continually in the dust.

The person chosen to lead the wagon train was elected on the basis of previous experience in leading wagon

28

On to Oregon

trains or knowledge of the terrain. The leader was usually paid. The train would travel only during daylight, with nights spent in camps along the way. The wagon leader, or captain, or master set the daily traveling pace and chose the camp spots.

The captain kept the wagon train as close as possible to the trail, no matter how sparse the grass was, or how much jouncing the pioneers experienced while following the well-worn tracks of previous wagons.

In the beginning, the wagon journey was fairly pleasant and exciting, although there was sorrow in leaving family members and former lives behind.

The advent of warm weather and the coming of green grass saw activities begin with feverish ardor. Wagons were put into condition for the long trek, supplies were gathered, teams were equipped, and preparations were completed.

Our tentative leaders were asked to meet and set the date for our departure, and arrange the plan of starting, for we knew that with a definite time set and a plan of procedure decided upon we could work toward them all the better.

Each community, neighborhood, or section was asked to start from its own home place and meet at a designated point, and there organize the train. The place for meeting was Nebraska City, where we would cross the Missouri River on a ferry boat. The word was passed that May 5, 1864 should be the time for our departure. Thereupon, all the wagons of our neighborhood, after the occupants had bidden a tearful good-bye to relatives, friends, and neighbors, turned toward the point for this great gathering of travelers to the unknown land of the western sun.

It took us five or six days to reach the rendezvous, my father going one day's journey with us. Parting from him was heart-breaking, and the hardest trial we had yet undergone. We knew that he wanted so much to go with us, and we knew, too, that if the War continued he would still have to make sacrifices and be subjected to groveling indignities. Now we must leave him alone to meet these trials unsupported. It seemed that I was giving him a last farewell, but through the goodness of my Heavenly Father I was permitted to meet him again in my old home after the lapse of twelve years, and to renew the associations so rudely broken.

When we reached our meeting place, others had arrived before us and others, still, were behind us. Our old friend, Colonel Flournoy, was here with a great number of cattle and mules. The ravages of War had dwindled his vast estate, and driven him from his home. He, like us, was seeking a new freedom in the West.

The camp near Nebraska City was in rather cramped quarters, and the pasturage for stock being not good, we decided to cross the river to the grassy plains on the other side in the hope of finding better grazing, and there to await the coming of the rest of the train. But we were disappointed as to the better grazing, for we found the vast extent of grassy plains literally covered with stock, both horses and cattle, under the care of herders. There were white tents and white covered wagons dotting the plains all around for miles, resembling a great city of miniature white buildings.

There were no settlements on the west side of the river at that time, and its only inhabitants were a few roving bands of Indians seeking to barter beaded work and buckskins to the emigrants.

This great aggregation of people, wagons, and livestock was a wonderful sight, and it indicated that there were other states as well as Missouri affected with the "Oregon fever," for there were wagon trains here from Iowa, Illinois, Nebraska, and perhaps from many other states. It has been estimated that ten thousand wagons crossed the Plains that year.

The spring was late and backward. The weather was cold and wet, and there was much discomfort in the camp. Fuel of any kind was very scarce. Trains were forming and starting out daily, but it was not considered a good policy to travel while the grass was so short and tender. The discomforts of camp were so great, and the people so impatient to be on their way, that they would remain here no longer than was necessary.

The rest of the train having arrived, a meeting was held and the expedition was organized. Freeman Goodman, who had twice before crossed the Plains, was elected captain. He was a man of firmness, but smooth and mild-tempered. All liked him and respected him greatly, and willingly submitted to his guidance. Thinking it best not to have too many bosses, the train elected no other officers. Soon we were in readiness to set out on our great adventure, with its attendant dangers and hardships, our goal the unknown West!

At the captain's command the wagons were placed in line, forming a long string, nearly a hundred in number, their white tops glistening in the sun. The horse-drawn wagons were placed in the lead; the ox teams behind, for they would travel more slowly and could not be rushed; the loose cattle and horses, of which there were a large number, still further behind, or more properly speaking, to one side, where they could graze along more slowly, attended by the young men.

And now the captain, on horseback, rides up and down the line, giving it a final inspection. All is in readiness. "Forward march!" Whips crack, the oxen bend their shoulders to the yoke, and amid hurrahs and cheers the train gets under way! "On to Oregon!" is the battle cry.

4

THE TRAIL

*We encountered many Indians on the Platte,
but none were hostile, and most of them were
inclined to be friendly.*

THE GREAT AMERICAN PRAIRIES once stretched from
the Mississippi to the Rockies and from Canada to Texas.
Before the coming of the railroads, these vast grasslands
were home to 60 to 70 million bison. The wagon trains
encountered the beginning of the prairie and their first buffalo near the Platte River.

There were three distinct belts of the prairie. The east-
ernmost third consisted of tall grasses, towering six to
twelve feet high. This Indian grass, bluestem, and switch-
grass could actually grow half an inch or more in a day.
An average of thirty inches of rain fell annually in tallgrass
country.

The next belt was called the mixed-grass prairie
because it combined short grasses and some tall grasses with mostly midsize grasses, such as needle grass and
wheat grass.

Closer to the Rockies, the prairies became short-grass
country, with blades six to twelve inches high. Short grasses, such as buffalo grass and blue grama, were the most

drought-tolerant of the prairie grasses. They grew in the rain shadow of the Rocky Mountains, where they received the least moisture.

Walt Whitman called the prairies "North America's characteristic landscape" because they covered one-ninth of the continent with an unbroken meadow as far as the eye could see. The prairies were where most pioneers first encountered the West, saw its true size and unique landscape, and felt the promise and newness beckon them.

In the twentieth century the prairies, once the greatest grasslands on Earth, were plowed under and corn and wheat fields took the place of grass. Today, many Americans are working to help the government replant and protect portions of this distinctive grassland landscape so that once again the true nature of the heartland can be seen and buffalo can roam and graze.

We were now fairly launched on our journey, traveling over the great Platte River plains. This was a large expanse of treeless country. Here was the summer range of the buffalo, and we cooked with buffalo "chips" [dung]. When we camped at evening the women and children went out with sacks and gathered the chips with which we cooked our meals. Sometimes the men helped in this task, but generally they had to attend first to getting the stock out to feed.

When we first began using this improvised fuel my sisters couldn't eat anything; their delicate appetites revolted at food prepared in this manner. But before we left the chip country they were only too glad to get food, regardless of how it had been cooked, and they later saw times when they would gladly have cooked with chips had they been able to get them. I had no qualms about such things, and I

Collecting buffalo chips for fuel

could gather the chips for fuel, cook with them, and eat heartily and poke fun at the girls over their squeamish appetites.

We had expected to be able to provide ourselves with fresh meat from wild game, but so great was the migration ahead of us that the game had been driven from the Trail, and our hunters were able to get but few buffalo or antelope, or any other game. This was a great disappointment to us, and increased the privations of the journey.

Day after day we journeyed up the Platte, with but few incidents to break the monotony in our travel. At evening we camped in units of relatives and friends. Though we had no wood for making big camp fires to gather around, some of our party had a big tent where we could go and spend a sociable evening. We had some musical instruments, such as the accordion and violin, and some very good musicians and singers. Music and song frequently filled the tent. I saw no card-playing, neither was there any carousing, or drunkenness, except on one occasion of which I shall speak later, leaving it to the reader to judge whether or not under the circumstances it might be excusable. Everyone brought along whiskey for emergencies, for it was then thought useful in many ways.

French trading posts along the way served to break the monotony of our travel. We could buy from the trader a few needed supplies, and we enjoyed watching his troop of children. The traders invariably had Indian wives.

Another colorful diversion that created excitement in our train was the passing of the mail stages. They swept along at high speed with six heavily-armed men at the driver's side and an equal number of armed guards on horseback speeding alongside the coach. Holdups and Indian raids were not infrequent, and often the stage, on arriving at the station, would find it in ashes, and the agent murdered. This was principally the work of marauding bands of Indians, led, perhaps, by a white renegade, but in some instances it was done by white men disguised as Indians. The stage always gave us warning if there was any danger from Indians.

Along the Platte we often saw large encampments of emigrants, waiting over from some cause or other, generally to give additional time for their stock to graze, for the grass was still short and pretty well grazed over.

36

One day we ourselves laid over near one of these large encampments. Some of the boys went over to visit them and incidentally to learn where they were from, always an interesting question among strangers. They learned that most of these people were from the southwestern part of Missouri, and that a Kansas train was also camped nearby. In this train was the wife and family of old John Brown of Osawatomie, the leader of the Harpers Ferry insurrection of whom it was popularly sung:

John Brown's body lies a-moldering in the grave.

Knowing that she was in such close proximity to so many Missourians, the lady was trying to keep her identity a secret, fearful of violence at their hands. She had either asked for an escort of federal soldiers to protect her on her way, or she expected to ask for them at the first hint of danger. But I know that she had nothing to fear from Missourians; they had affairs of greater moment on their minds than molesting a helpless woman and her children.

I never heard whether or not Mrs. Brown got the escort, but I later learned that she had gotten safely through to California where she spent the remainder of her life and raised her family amid peaceful scenes.

While camped one night along the Platte, we experienced a most unusual happening—a very annoying one, too, while it lasted; but out of it grew a rather amusing incident which afforded some of us quite a bit of merriment.

Just about dark, before we had finished our suppers, we were suddenly overrun by an army of bugs. I never learned of what species they were, nor whence they came, but in size they were about like beetles; and in number, apparently, like the grasshoppers of old that plagued Pharaoh in behalf of the Israelites. They came swarming into everything. I never saw so many bugs in my life before, nor since either, for that matter. There were bugs everywhere—in our pots and pans, in our tea kettles and coffee pots, in our dishes and water pails, in our food, in our faces, in our hair; yes, in our mouths, if we so much as dared to open them to eat or talk.

The lights of our fires seemed to attract them, and they came in such hordes that we decided to put out all lights, and endure the calamity in darkness. We did not even dare light a lantern to see how to get into our beds, but retired in the dark, hoping thus to avoid having them for bed-fellows, feeling that sleeping under such circumstances would be uncomfortable.

5
LOST ON THE PRAIRIE!

Besides, there was an element of danger in separating ourselves from the train in an unknown country. The element of danger, perhaps, was one reason the walks were so attractive to me.

THE FAMILIAR IMAGE of a wagon train with its white-topped Conestoga wagons arranged in a tight circle, surrounded by attacking Indians on horseback, is more fiction than fact. In the 1860s, cholera and accidents killed more pioneers than Indians did. Yet the fear of Indian raids was so pervasive among the emigrants that rumors of attacks circulated almost daily. In addition, many of the emigrants brought with them from the East their old ideas about and attitudes toward the Indians. Most of these attitudes had been formed by reading popular stories and novels that stressed the horrors of Indian warfare.

Basically, the difficulties between the Indians and emigrants can be traced to misunderstandings and lack of respect shown to the Indians by the settlers. The Indians of the Great Plains were trying to keep their homeland while the settlers were trying to seize it. Broken promises, brutality, and the destruction of nearly all the buffalo marked these years of conflict between the Indians and the land-hungry emigrants.

*Attacks on emigrant trains were popular subjects
for artists, and their dramatic illustrations
increased the settlers' fears.*

There is little indication in Arabella's memoir that she
or the other members of the wagon train understood the
Indians' predicament. The emigrants were more concerned
with the day-to-day problems of feeding themselves and
their livestock, dealing with the weather and the terrain,
and relieving the monotony of the slow-paced, daily travel routine.

Each day after breaking camp the pioneers traveled until they stopped for their noontime dinner and a brief rest. After the "nooning" period they traveled until early evening. Any change from the routine was welcome but sometimes dangerous.

In our train were quite a number of little boys and girls who loved action. Sometimes for diversion, I would gather them up in the morning, form a company of little soldiers and start on ahead of the wagons. Frequently we would travel several miles on ahead before the children would complain of being tired. They had stocks for guns and used anything they could get for swords. Some of the children had brought along horns and Jew's harps, and other musical playthings. So, we had lots of noise of a musical nature when we started on our marches in the mornings.

One morning we took a cutoff path that led us considerable distance from the main traveled road. In fact, we were out of sight of the train. Looking ahead we saw an Indian brave coming toward us full tilt, riding Indian fashion with his pony on the run. A bow and quiver of arrows hung at his side, and his long, black hair was flying in the wind.

We could do nothing but stand and gaze at him. The children all huddled up close to me, but made no outcry. When the Indian came quite near us he stopped suddenly, held out his hand toward me, and in a guttural voice greeted me. I shook hands with him, then he wanted to shake hands with all the children. Some gave him their hands, a little reluctantly, however, and some wouldn't; but little Tommy, when he saw that I gave him my hand, walked up and offered the Indian his hand, too.

Using motions for speech, the Indian tried to ask where our train was. I pointed toward the road.

"Ki-yi?" he inquired, meaning "way off?"

I asked him if there were any more Indians coming. He shook his head. "No Indian." Then I asked how soon we would come to the road.

"Soon," he replied. All this talking was done mostly by signs.

"Bye-bye, clatawa." said the Indian, meaning "Must be going," and off he went in the same manner as he came.

By this time the children were over their fright, and we hurried to overtake the train. When the children told their mothers about the Indian, it was decided that I must never take the children out of sight of the train any more. And I didn't. This ended our marches. We were now entering Indian territory, where hostile Indians might be encountered.

Some of the mothers scolded me for taking the children on the cutoff path; others laughed about it, and my brother-in-law said that Tommy and I were much alike, that neither of us knew enough to fear danger.

These cutoff paths were by-paths or foot-paths made by people traveling single file on horseback or afoot. They were too narrow for wagon travel. Usually they ran diagonally to the main road and were traveled principally by hunters, prospectors, and Indians; also by the loose people of the train who could be spared from tasks. The paths were nice to walk in, were free from dust, and usually they led to all the nice, little shaded nooks along the way. Sometimes they skirted little ravines with running water, but seldom did they leave the main road for any distance. There was always danger of meeting Indians—at least we thought there was—but the one instance I mentioned was the only occasion on which we met an Indian in these places.

The cutoff paths really saved quite a distance in a day's walk, and I loved to travel them. It was nicer to walk than to ride; walking broke the monotony of that long, drawn-out train of wagons, and it added a charm to the road, which otherwise was missing. Rarely could I get any of the mature people of the train to go with me. Several young girls went occasionally, but their mothers objected, for fear we would meet with danger. There were several young men in the train whose company might have been acceptable, but a rule or code of ethics forbade young couples of opposite sex to leave the train for long walks. And no one seemed to have the temerity or the inclination to break this rule. We had courtships, to be sure, among the young folks, and one wedding en route; two other weddings took place as soon as we reached our destination, but never a whisper of scandal did we ever hear, although we were a jolly crowd of young folks.

One day, farther on our journey, we started out from a noon camp near one of these cutoff paths. It descended a little hill toward a green skirt of timber. I was sure a stream of water flowed through the place, and it looked so inviting that I persuaded my sister, the mother of a little babe, and another woman, the wife of our train captain, who also had a nursing babe, to go with me for a walk.

And we surely enough had a walk that afternoon! Very enjoyable at first. Our path led us down along a cool, trickling stream, flowing between low, mossy banks decked with little, star-like flowers, over which hung green boughs of trees, which made our pathway a shady bower.

For two or three hours we traveled on and on, feeling no uneasiness. Then we began to notice that the hills were getting higher, and that we were traveling upstream and getting into a deep canyon. The hills closed in at times, then widened out again, but not sufficiently to afford us a perspective of the country through which we were passing. The train was nowhere in sight or hearing and from the wildness of the country we grew apprehensive that danger might lurk unseen on all sides.

We came to one place of perhaps an acre or so of level ground, thickly covered with quaking aspens, but fortunately for our peace of mind, the trail avoided this place and led around the foot of the hill. By this time we were becoming uneasy and perhaps a little frightened. Slipping along very quietly, we heard a rustling among the bushes, and stopped to listen. We heard the same kind of noise in another place, and then realized that more than one creature was stirring in the thicket near at hand.

We didn't know just what to do. There was no way for us to hide and escape being seen, so we just stood still. The noise continued; it seemed a slow, deliberate moving about, and I judged that it couldn't be Indians, so I decided to take a peep to see what it was. "Oh, don't, Belle" said both women, in low voices tense with excitement. But I told them it was best to know what it was.

Creeping up very cautiously, I parted the bushes, and behold! What do you think I saw? A big, fat ox! I let the women know what it was and, made bold by my discovery, I slipped back and took another look. I counted six big, fine oxen! Some emigrant, doubtless, had lost his team, and the oxen, finding excellent pasturage, had grown sleek and fat in this solitude. Their loss must have been a calamity to the owner, who, unless he had some fill-ins, was rendered dependent upon his fellow-travelers. In some cases emigrants brought along extra stock for just such emergencies.

Feeling much relieved, we hurried on, but we traveled quite a distance before the trail took us up and out on level ground again, where it turned toward the traveled road. It was now growing late in the day. We were very tired from our long walk and the excitement and uneasiness we had undergone. The two women were becoming uneasy about their babies, and they soon began to look at me as the author of their misfortunes.

When we at last reached the road, another source of uneasiness confronted us. None of the wagons were in sight, neither ahead nor behind us, and we could see for a considerable distance in either direction. We decided to keep to the cutoff path, thinking we might come in ahead of the train in a short time. But alas! In this we were mistaken, for we traveled on and on, and still could not see the wagons. The sun went down and we knew the train had camped somewhere for the night. We could do nothing but go on.

On reaching higher ground we looked across the country in the direction of the road and saw three campfires about a mile apart. We were sure that these indicated the camps of our train, but the question was, which one was ours? The middle one being the largest, we decided it must be that of our contingent; so we started for it, going straight across the country.

By this time darkness had covered the plains, and to make matters worse, the country was rough and uneven. Our travel was slow, for we had to select our way with care, and we were oh, so tired. Finally we saw two lights coming in our direction. Feeling sure that someone was hunting for us, we went to meet the light bearers. They proved to be the husbands of the two women, and very irate husbands they were, too! They scolded us and said the babies were making the welkin [heavens] ring, howling for their suppers, when they left.

The men then and there laid down an ultimatum to their wives, that henceforth and forever they were to refrain from leaving the train in this manner. I spoke up: "You needn't worry on that score. You couldn't hire them to do it again." I told them to scold me, and not their wives, for I was the culprit. We had given the poor men such a fright that I could not blame them for scolding, but it seemed to me to be an occasion more for rejoicing than for harsh words, and when we reached the camp there was, indeed, quite a rejoicing.

This ended my by-path walks, and really, I had no desire for another, so nerve-racking this one had proved.

6
RIVER CROSSING

The hands of the men who helped us onto the
boats were shaking; their eyes were downcast
and their faces pale and drawn. This was a
moment for fortitude.

PERHAPS AS MANY AS 10 PERCENT of the people who
attempted the Oregon Trail died along the way, mostly
from wagon accidents, drownings, and illnesses. River
crossings were particularly dangerous in the early years
of the Western migration. Equally dreaded were violent
storms that typically struck the Platte River region of
Nebraska and Wyoming. These horrific, thunder-and-light-
ning storms could last for days and cause enormous discomfort and fear. Floods, hail, and wind threatened the
pioneers. But lasting out a storm was a minor problem
when compared to crossing a treacherous river, swollen
from constant spring rains. Getting all the people, animals,
and equipment across challenged the pioneers' strength
and courage. The pioneers depended on word of mouth
and the knowledge of their leaders to tell them where to
cross a river and how to do it, but they were the ones who
had to assume the risks.

At the end of six weeks we had traveled about six or seven hundred miles. We were still on the south side of the Platte River, about forty miles below Julesburg, at which point we expected to cross on the government ferry.

For a few days we had been having threatening weather, and we heard that it had rained hard in the mountains. We went into camp one night on a little sandy knoll, with low ground or a swale between us and the banks of the river. Our camping place was, in reality, a low-water island.

We still had our daily task of gathering buffalo chips for fuel, but they were now getting scarce as so many were gathering them. Occasionally some of the boys found a few sticks of driftwood, which helped the fuel situation somewhat. At this camping place we were fortunate to find some large weeds of last year's growth. By constantly replenishing the fires with these weeds, we succeeded in doing our cooking very nicely.

On this particular night it began to rain, and it rained hard. We realized that the June rains, which we had been dreading, were upon us. Next morning everything looked very gloomy, and the little weeds, though wet and few, were the only fuel we had for cooking our breakfasts.

While we were eating, one of the men came rushing up and shouting, "Get to moving quickly! The river is rising fast, coming in great waves!" Ah, then there was hurrying to and fro, for the water was running down the swale and we were on an island! Some of the men, already having their horses in, used them to take out the wagons, but the horses had to swim with the last wagon and some of the provisions were soaked. We were thankful the discovery was made so

Crossing the flooded Platte River

soon, otherwise the camp would have been inundated, and the train in a serious situation.

There's an old saying that "It never rains but it pours," and this day our troubles began. It rained. And kept on raining. The stage reported rumors of trouble at the ferry. Our captain, on investigation, found that the boat had broken loose some days before, and so much time had been lost in recovering it that it was now three weeks behind with the crossings. Feed was short and the stock were getting thin. Everyone was discouraged. Conditions were bound

49

to be worse up at the ferry, where thousands were congregated.

Thereupon, the men of our train held a conference, and decided that, while it was bad enough where we were, it would be folly to go on up to the ferry. In their perplexity, someone suggested the feasibility of making boats of the wagon bodies and crossing the river in them. It may have been the captain who suggested it, as it was something none in our train had ever tried before. However, it seemed to give promise of relief, and on deciding to try it, everyone went to work with a will.

Six of the best constructed wagon boxes were selected, one of ours being of the number. These were unloaded and their contents piled into tents. The women, using pitch and the tar used for axle grease in those days, caulked the seams and soon had the wagon boxes watertight. Then, lashing two of them together and fastening one behind in order to balance the craft, they made an improvised scow which they felt would be sufficiently buoyant to carry a wagon across. Two of these queer craft were thus constructed. Some, fearing to attempt crossing in this manner, went on up the river, while others, not caring to try it, dropped behind for a few days to give their loose stock a chance to graze, saying that we had been driving too fast for them, anyway. I do not remember the exact number of wagons that waited to cross on this improvised ferry, but I think it was twenty.

We had now been in camp four days and every day we had some rain, but so far, no hail. About ten o'clock on the fourth day it was announced that the boats were ready for loading. The men had planned to take some of the women and children across with every load. Now the question arose: Who should go first? These turbulent waters looked dangerous. The river had spread out of its banks and was full a quarter of a mile wide. None of us had ever seen boats so constructed, and naturally we were apprehensive as to their performance in these turgid waters.

Who, of the women and children, should be the first to make the trial? I reasoned with myself that I could better be spared than anyone else in the train, in case disaster overtook the strange crafts, and I volunteered to go first. To this my sisters strenuously objected. But I said "Yes, I will go. Someone has to be first." When they saw that they could not dissuade me, both said they would go with me, as their husbands were helping with the boats. Then a brave little woman, with two small children, volunteered to go with the other boat. She said, if it were God's will, she would drown with her children. Two young girls then came forward to go on the boat with her.

The improvised boats did splendidly. They didn't even wobble. Either we had good oarsmen, or the good Lord was helping them, for we were landed safely on the opposite bank of the swollen river. With lighter hearts the men went back for another load. The other women were now ready and eager to go.

On the second trip the men brought bedding and tents sufficient to shelter us, for it looked like rain again. The rest of the day these clumsy barges plied back and forth across the river, bringing their precious cargoes of goods and people. By night, half the women and children had been transferred in safety across the swollen waters.

Next day the rain continued, in showers, but it was not accompanied by heavy winds, and by two o'clock all the women and children had been ferried across in safety. This accomplished, a great strain was lifted from these poor men who had keenly felt the burden of their responsibility. That afternoon they were able to bring over several of the wagons with their covers intact, which made shelter for the women and children.

The elements thus far had favored our crossing.

The last two days there had been only gentle showers, not sufficient to interfere greatly with the work, and the men made satisfactory progress in getting the equipment across the river. Many of the wagons and nearly all the livestock were yet to be brought across, however.

This night the rain began in earnest, accompanied by high winds, hail, and lightning. Next day the storm came on in its fury. Lightning struck all around us. One man, standing in the door of his tent, was killed. Two horses nearby were struck down, but being only stunned, were soon revived by the rain. About the same hour a baby girl was born in one of the wagon boxes, which had been placed on the ground. Its birth was premature, brought on, I presume, by the fright of the mother in the fearful conditions surrounding us. The wonder of it is that the child lived, and traveled with us during the remainder of the journey.

But the poor stricken man, and his family. This was a sad case. They were from Iowa and had joined our train, from another, only a short time previously. They were in hard circumstances. Their wagon, old and rickety, was in no condition for such a journey. Their team consisted of three yoke of cows, which was fortunate, as the cows gave milk for the children, of which there were four—one, however, being a girl of sixteen.

The mother was utterly dazed by the terrible catastrophe, and seemed to be unable to think or to speak. The sixteen-year-old girl was frantic with grief. There was little we could do to assuage her grief. The women of the train took the children in charge, and the men dug a grave.

There was nothing from which to make a coffin, but one man in the train had a trunk which he emptied and kindly donated. After removing one end of it, they placed the dead man's head and shoulders in this rude coffin, spread a white handkerchief over his face, wrapped a blanket around the remainder of his body, and lowered him into a very muddy grave, for the rain was still falling. A short prayer was offered, then the grave was filled in, and there they left him to await the Resurrection Morn. All during this sad scene the mother took no notice, still stunned, perhaps mercifully so, but the daughter continued frantic until she became exhausted. We put her to bed, hoping that sleep would relieve her.

We went back to our camps gloomily, chilled and hungry. We had no fuel for making fires for cooking; we had eaten nothing but the dry bread and crackers which we had brought with us. We had milk for the children, however, as there were several cows giving milk, and they were milked as regularly as possible. How the mothers managed to keep the children warm, I could not say, but I presume they kept the smaller ones in bed, wrapped in blankets. We had put on our heavy, home-made woolen clothes such as we usually wore in winter.

Next day the weather was somewhat better, and the men resumed their labor of getting the wagons across. The task was practically finished by night.

Now began the task of getting the livestock across. During the storm they had given the herders no end of trouble. They had stampeded so much during the hail and lightning that some of them were not found for two or three days, and might have been lost altogether had not the French trader from a post about two miles below sent his Indians to hunt them. This was indeed a kindness to us, and the Indians were very reasonable in their charges.

The cattle were hungry and on the move continually hunting feed, of which they found a very insufficient amount. But the real trouble began when the boys tried to drive them into the river. When driven near it, they began milling, and then broke and scattered in all directions. This performance they repeated over and over, until the men went across in the boats to help the boys.

During all this cold, stormy weather, the boys looking after the stock were up all night and day in the rain and without sufficient food. As there was no fuel for making fires, either for warming or drying themselves or for cooking, they were allowed some whiskey to keep up their spirits. One of the boys— Benton Hubbard, Little Benty, we called him—took a little too much for his own good, and it made him reckless. Old Buck, the leader of the cattle, was causing all the trouble. After a particularly provoking demonstration, Benty said to the other boys, "I bet I can make Old Buck take the water next time!"

Just as they got the cattle to the water's edge, Benty jumped from his horse onto Old Buck's back and caught him by the horns. This scared the old fellow out of his wits. His sole thought was to get rid of that thing on his back, and to get away from the yelling, whooping and cracking of whips. Plunging straight into the water, he struck for the farther shore, Benty riding him right through. The others followed, and soon the whole herd was swimming the Platte, headed for our side.

Benty was a great favorite of the camp, and when the women saw that it was he who had done this brave but reckless deed, they gave him a mighty ovation. We did not know at that time that whiskey had bolstered up his courage to the point of such recklessness, but as the end seemed to justify the means, we would have been just as enthusiastic anyway, for they had been struggling for three days with those cattle, trying to get them across. Benty's method, while novel, was both effective and spectacular, and it was the first exhibition of bulldogging we had ever seen.

The horses gave but little trouble, and their crossing would have been without incident had not Benty's horse, while swimming, tangled his feet with the bridle reins. To relieve him Benty jumped into the water, and in so doing, released his hold. The horse, thus freed, struck out alone, leaving Benty to swim. Already fatigued, Benty soon became so badly chilled that he could not make it, but he managed to reach a little sand bar half way across. Witnessing his struggle, and seeing that Benty was in dire straits, the men on shore launched a boat to hasten to his rescue. Just then a storm of wind, rain, and hail came up with such violence that the boat could not face it. The storm was soon over, however, and the men pulled out. Benty was still alive when they reached him, but was so badly chilled that he was helpless. When we saw the men lift Benty into the boat, we women on shore thought that brave little Benty was dead, and nearly all of us broke down and cried. His little sweetheart was distracted, and for a time there was much lamentation. Little Benty was an orphan boy and he was very popular, not only with the women, but with the men as well, for he was always energetic and willing to do his part.

As soon as they reached shore, the men wrapped Benty in blankets and put him to bed, first plying him with more whiskey and bathing him with it until blood circulation had again started. There was yet an anxious group of women waiting around the tent to hear how his chances for recovery were, and when it was announced that Benty was out of danger, there was great rejoicing and thanksgiving in the camp.

In the meantime, some of the men had found a small amount of driftwood and brought it to the camp. After the storm ceased, they trimmed off the wet outer layers, broke up some empty cracker boxes for kindling, and managed to make a pretty good fire—the best we had since the storms caught us. We made some coffee for Benty and the other boys, which was better for them than whiskey. We prepared some warm food for them, the first they had been able to get for several days, which cheered them considerably after all the hardships they had undergone.

The storm that caught Benty was our last. The skies began to clear, and the next day was warm and sunshiny. Our two weeks' rain was over.

The poor woman whose husband was killed by lightning was yet in a dazed condition, but the daughter was becoming her normal self. The men of the train did the best they could to put their wagon in shape for travel, and a young man was persuaded to take charge of it, for the family was in no shape to continue the journey otherwise.

Next morning we turned our backs to the turgid waters of the Platte, the scene of so much sorrow and discomfort. With renewed courage and greater hope we resumed our journey westward.

7

CROSSING THE PLAINS

A solemn hush was in the air, and we talked in subdued tones. Guards were stationed around the camp, and we prepared for bed—some to sleep, but not mothers!

FROM ITS STARTING POINT at Independence, Missouri, at the bend of the Missouri River, the long and difficult Oregon Trail led northwest to Fort Kearny, Nebraska, on the Platte River. This fort was the first one built to protect emigrants along the Oregon Trail. After Fort Kearny, the trail ran straight west along the Platte, and its north fork ran into southern Wyoming. The countryside got drier and more rugged as the train got closer to Chimney Rock, a 470-foot spire that was one of the most anticipated landmarks along the Trail. Independence Rock, a huge block of granite on the north bank of the Sweetwater River in Wyoming, was another important landmark. If they were on schedule, the pioneers hoped to reach Independence Rock by Independence Day. It was vital that the wagon train keep on schedule. Any delay could mean that the whole group would be caught in the high mountains when winter set in. Exhausted or sick animals unable to keep up the pace were either shot or simply left to die. Sometimes the captain forced families whose wagons could not be

Chimney Rock, on the North Platte
River, in western Nebraska

repaired on the trail to leave the train at the nearest army fort.

Nearly 100 miles past Independence Rock, the emigrant trains crossed the Rocky Mountains at South Pass, a 7,550-foot-high mountain pass that marked the Continental Divide and was the easiest route across the Rockies. The climb up to the pass was so gentle that many pioneers were surprised to find out that they had crossed the Rocky Mountains and were on the other side before they realized it.

After crossing the Rockies at South Pass, the Trail led to the Green River Valley at Fort Bridger, Wyoming, then turned northwest to Fort Hall in the Snake River area and on to Fort Boise, Idaho. After Boise, the pioneers crossed the Blue Mountains to Walla Walla, Washington. Then they traveled down the Columbia River to Fort Vancouver and the Willamette River Valley of Oregon.

Pioneers such as Arabella and her family, traveling the Great Plains in the 1860s, had to be on guard in case of Indian attacks. As more and more emigrants settled on the plains, the Indians—particularly the Sioux and the Cheyenne—began to defend their hunting grounds by attacking the settlers and the wagon trains. The United States army responded to these attacks by sending more cavalry to the line of western forts. In the period from just before the Civil War to shortly before the end of the century, more than 1,000 battles occurred between the army and the Indians. Casualties were estimated to include 2,571 soldiers and civilians and at least 5,500 Indians.

With hopeful hearts we started on again, the nightmare of the Platte fading in the light of other scenes and prospective perils. Mile after mile we traveled on with patient slowness, till the trail seemed never-ending, wearing on man and beast. Day after day we continued up the North Platte, but making slow progress in order to give our leg-weary cattle time to feed and rest. The weather was fair, and the grass was lush where it was not grazed too closely. Such streams as we encountered were now at low water and gave us little trouble in crossing. There were few landmarks to blaze our way, and only the wagon ruts and cattle trails to guide us.

Knowing the names of some of the larger and more noted rivers on ahead, we were somewhat apprehensive, from past experience, as to their crossing. These water courses and a few landmarks, such as Chimney Rock, gave us the only idea of the distance to be traveled and of the progress we were making.

We could see Chimney Rock, in western Nebraska, looming up in the distance ahead of us for some days before we reached it. This noted landmark created much interest, especially among the young folks of the train, and as we drew alongside it, all of them not otherwise engaged, rushed out with their knives to carve their names on the soft rock. This, we heard, was a practice of the Trail. I went with the others, and we all cut our names in the rock. As high as the best climber among us could go, were names of people who had sought a diversion in this pastime, and we found it of much interest to read the names already carved. It was our ambition to put our names above the rest, but having no way to make footsteps, we were unable to reach very high. Although we carved our names laboriously and patiently, with what skill we possessed, I am doubtful that any of them are legible today.

This huge column of rock, shaped somewhat like a chimney as its name would suggest, was composed of a grayish-white sedimentary substance, scarcely hard enough to be called rock yet harder than the material that surrounded it. Apparently it had once been a high mound, or a fragment of the white bluffs of the Platte, but it had been sloughed off by erosion until there remained only a high, slim column resembling a chimney standing out amid ruins of an old castle.

A few more days' travel brought us to Fort Laramie on the plains of eastern Wyoming. On our arrival we found the Fort in a great state of excitement. Indians had attacked a Kansas emigrant train about three days' journey beyond. They had killed three men of the train, wounded another, and captured three women, carrying them off as prisoners. The train had dispatched a runner to the Fort for assistance, and a detachment of soldiers was rushed to the scene of disorder, followed by the army ambulance and other conveyances. The wounded man was brought to the Fort with the arrow still sticking in his back, and the women and children of the train were also brought to the Fort for safety. While we were here a report came that the soldiers had overtaken the Indians some miles beyond the place of the attack, and that a battle was in progress.

To the train in general, this news caused great anxiety. But to me it was romance, and I pictured the gallant array of soldiers dashing over the boundless plains, eager to avenge the slain! I heard, in my mind, the shouts of the boys in blue as they swept down to battle. . . . O, to be a man and to ride to the defense of the helpless!

Next day we drove on. We met the army ambulance coming in about ten o'clock that morning, with about a dozen soldiers as guards. They were bringing in three badly wounded soldiers attended by the army surgeon. They told us that in the battle the Indians had killed three of the soldiers and wounded three others. The Indians had been routed, and a running fight had followed. How many of the Indians had been killed was unknown, for they always carried their dead away, if possible. The women captives had not been recovered, but the soldiers were still in pursuit, and it was felt that the women would be rescued.

The third night brought us to the scene of this attack on the emigrant train, and we had to camp in this gruesome place. Scattered here and there were the partly burned wagons, with their contents trampled in the dust and ashes. Any worthwhile provi-

*An 1867 photograph shows a treaty negotiation
between government commissioners and Indian
chiefs at Fort Laramie. Sadly, many treaty
promises to the Indians were later broken.*

sions had been taken, of course, when the train
resumed its journey. Three fresh graves lay side by
side, where the soldiers had buried the slain men—
grim reminders of what we too might have met, or,
for that matter, might still meet, before our goal was
reached.

The captain, realizing that we now were in dangerous territory, decided to maintain greater vigilance; but as we traveled on and had no more Indian scares, our fears subsided and we regained our usual cheerfulness and hopefulness as we thought of that Western goal.

We were following the general course of the Oregon Trail, which wound its way over mountain and plain, its many deviations converging at South Pass, Wyoming, which, in a general way, marked the divide between the Atlantic and Pacific slopes.

In our journey across Wyoming, which we had entered near Fort Laramie, we crossed Chugwater Creek, a rather insignificant little stream, but one of much historic interest in the early settlement of that territory. It is mentioned incidentally in Parkman's story of Chief Pontiac, although hundreds of miles from the scenes of his activities. [Francis Parkman, a nineteenth-century historian, traveled a portion of the Oregon Trail in 1846 and wrote of his experiences in the widely read *The Oregon Trail*. In a later book, *History of the Conspiracy of Pontiac*, he wrote a full account of the great Ottawa chief's struggle against the British in the French and Indian War.]

We crossed the renowned Laramie River not far from where it is joined by the North Laramie, only a few miles from the present city of Wheatland. Our course took us somewhere near the location of what is now Casper, the oil city of Wyoming. Thence, across a long stretch, mile after mile, to the South Pass.

Independence Rock was another landmark by which we measured the distance traveled. Anticipation of reaching this noted spot held our interest, but to us it was less attractive than Chimney Rock in Nebraska had been. The rock itself was composed of much harder substance, and could not easily be cut with a knife, but it bore some names which we concluded were cut with a chisel. We young folks who had left the train to visit the rock did not remain long, and when we caught up with the wagons, were not so tired as we thought we might have been.

Our captain told us that when we passed through the South Pass, we could consider ourselves in the Western Territory. One woman asked how far it was to Oregon now.

"Oh," he answered, "we are a long way off. We are not half way yet."

When we reached South Pass we were very much disappointed in the topography of the country. We had expected to find a rough, rugged, mountainous district, over which we would pass with difficulty. Instead we found a long, smooth, gradual climb, seemingly not reaching a very high altitude. Later we became acquainted with real western mountains, and by comparison the terrain of South Pass did not seem like mountains at all.

We next entered the Sweetwater country, a very desolate expanse with brackish water and poor grass, and then on to the Big Sandy. We had no trouble crossing any of these stretches as the waters were low. We would soon be approaching the Green River, after which we hoped to have more pleasant traveling, as the reports we had heard of that section of the journey were more favorable.

8
A TRAIL EXPERIENCE

On the Sublette cutoff—I'm not sure of the exact location—we came to a very forbidding country with loose alkaline or mineralized soil. Here we encountered high winds and dusty roads and our hands and faces became roughened and chapped, sometimes to the point of cracking and bleeding.

AFTER THEY TRAVELED through the Rocky Mountains at the Continental Divide, most pioneers were exhausted and thin. Yet the most demanding terrain was still in front of them and had to be crossed at the time when their supplies of water, food, and energy were dwindling. For many, the rapid depletion of their supplies was the deciding factor in choosing which route to follow for the remainder of the journey. Those who felt they had enough resources to complete the long journey to the Pacific Coast stayed on the main Oregon Trail, crossing the Blue Mountains and floating their wagons by canoe and raft down the Columbia River to Oregon City, the capital of Oregon at the time. Others were forced to shorten the distance by taking cutoff routes, or changing their final destinations. Unfortunately, the most recent information about the routes was sometimes inaccurate, but the travelers didn't have any way of knowing that. When the decision about the route to follow was made, there was often no turning back. The popular alternate routes were the Sublette cutoff, which eventual-

Crossing the Rocky Mountains

ly led back to the main trail, and the Applegate Trail, and the Barlow Road, both of which led into Oregon's Willamette River Valley, but avoided the first set of difficult mountains to cross—the Blue Mountains.

On all the trails, warring Indians remained a threat to the emigrants' safety because of the depletion of the buffalo and antelope herds, and the Indians' anger at the settlers' appropriation of lands where Indians lived and hunted. Sometimes wagon-train travelers were caught in the middle of an attack of one tribe on another. Arabella's description of an encounter with a Pawnee party demonstrates the lack of understanding that the emigrants and Indians had for each other's society and the fears that shaped their actions.

*F*ew, if any of the emigrant trains that started across the plains remained intact; rather, they divided at various places along the journey. Some went north to reach the newly discovered mining territory, others branched off for one purpose or another, some finding permanent locations or making enforced stops along the way.

We had taken the Sublette cutoff and were not on the main branch. Our train also had divided. No more than half of the wagons we had at the beginning were still with us. It was necessary to spread out in this manner to obtain stock feed. Often we had to drive the stock two or three miles from camp for pasturage. The inaccessibility of feed necessarily made progress very slow. Eventually all cutoffs and by-ways led back to the main trail.

The first water we came to was a clear, nice-looking spring. Without testing it, the first wagoneer to arrive, seeing what appeared to be good water, unyoked his oxen, and they rushed to the spring to drink. Before he had gotten his wheel team unyoked he noticed something wrong with the first team. By this time others had arrived and were unyoking their cattle in order to give them water. Someone happened to find a sign marked POISON, which had been trampled in the dust, but the discovery was too late to save the cattle which had already drunk the water. Some of the people had already taken a drink before the warning was found. I among others.

Two of the oxen died, and all of us who had drunk from the spring were ill a few days, but no one died from its effects. The sign informed us that there was good water five miles farther on. This caused us a long drive that day to reach a watering place, and there was much suffering among the sick people before we could make camp. The poor, sick oxen, dragging their heavy loads, plodded along in that interminably long five miles to the good water.

Along the route of the Bitter Creek and Sweetwater countries we found travel very disagreeable; grass and good drinking water were both scarce, and we were glad indeed when our captain announced that we would soon leave the Sweetwater country and come to Green River. There remained, however, a twenty-four hour drive with no water for the stock, and only what water we could carry for ourselves.

Under the circumstances, the men thought it a good plan for us to lay over during the greater part of the day, and prepare enough food to last us during the long drive, and make a night journey of it. Accordingly, the stock was put out to graze and rest during the day under the care of a large detachment of the men. Our best hunters went out to try to get some wild game for fresh meat. We were practically out of the buffalo range, but we were in antelope country and there was other small game some distance back from the trail. Others of the men remained about camp to do the chores, grease the wagons, and put them in traveling condition. Everybody about camp was very busy making ready for the night drive.

The water all along this section was very unwholesome, and several head of cattle died from drinking it. A cow had died the night before, and her carcass was lying behind us about a hundred yards from camp. During the forenoon one of our party chanced to glance in that direction and saw a large group of Indians gathered around the carcass of the dead cow. We saw at once they were a band of warriors, covered in warpaint and feathers.

The sudden, silent appearance of the Indians petrified us. No one screamed. No one moved or made any outcry. We simply stood and looked at them, realizing we were at their mercy. Soon several of them approached us, and when quite near, made signs of friendliness. One, who could speak a few words of English, made us understand that they had come to ask for the dead cow. Our men tried to tell them that the cow had died from poison and was unfit to eat, but the brave shook his head, saying, "Oh, no!" Of course, we were glad to give it to them.

The Indians told us they were not fighting the whites, but were a Pawnee tribe fighting the Sioux, and were now out on a raid. They were about sixty in number.

Having acquired peaceable possession of the dead cow, most of the Indians bent themselves to the task of removing it. But about twenty of them hung around our camp, asking for the things we were cooking.

During their visit one old warrior took a fancy to my red hair, which was braided in two strands and hanging down my back. He wanted to strike up a trade for it, and offered me a pony for my hair. I refused. Thereupon he took a looking glass, which was suspended from his neck, and a lot of other trin-

A water source along the trail

kets he had about him, and put them in a pile and made signs to say that he would trade them all for my hair. I shook my head, and tried to show him that there was no way of removing my hair. He understood, and unsheathing a great big hunting knife, he made motions to show me that he could cut it off with the knife. By motions I protested that he might cut my neck, but he indicated he would put the back of the knife to my neck and cut from me, and thus not hurt me.

My brother-in-law, who was standing by watching the performance, was having a bad case of nerves, and being apprehensive of trouble, said, "Belle, perhaps you had better let him cut it off and take it. You know we are in no position to argue just now." At this point my sister made a strategic move and offered the old brave a dried apple pie. He took it off to eat it, and being engrossed in the pie, forgot about my hair, I presume; at any rate, he didn't come back any more. That pie had saved my hair!

The Indians left us about noon, having either eaten the dead cow or prepared the meat for carrying with them. Anyway, we were much relieved to see the last of them. When the men brought back the stock they were astonished to learn about our visitors, and much relieved to find us all safe.

We all began to hustle now to get ready for the night's drive. At about four o'clock in the afternoon we resumed our journey and traveled all night without incident. Stopping next morning to rest our stock, but not unhitching, we ate a light breakfast and soon were on our way. We reached the Green River country about three o'clock that afternoon. The night's drive had not only saved time, but had relieved the stock. We found good spring water high up a mountainside and the camp site, though poorly located so far as our personal comfort was concerned, afforded us good water and plenty of feed for the stock, and that was our greatest concern. Next morning we crossed the divide, and that night we arrived in the Green River Valley, where we found plenty of wood and much good feed for the animals. From now on, our travel would be far more pleasant and comfortable.

9
UP AND DOWN
AND ACROSS

*We women thought it took greater courage to
cross in the wagons than it did to cross in the
boats. It was terrifying to see the horses and
cattle struggling in the water harnessed to the
wagons, having to swim the deep, swift river,
and we were thankful when the ordeal was
past.*

IT'S BEEN SAID that if it weren't for the ox the West might
not have been settled, at least not by pioneers traveling
overland. In the eighteenth and nineteenth centuries, farmers compared horses and oxen the way their counterparts
in the twentieth century compared horses and tractors. An
ox could pull far heavier weights than a horse could, and it
was not unusual for a team of two oxen to pull 600 pounds.
Getting a fully loaded Conestoga wagon up hills, across
rivers, and down steep inclines was never easy for the pioneers. But it was possible when the whole group could
work together and combine their muscle power with that
of oxen teams.

An ox is a castrated bull over the age of four that has
been trained to work. Oxen do not need elaborate har-
nessing as they respond to spoken commands and will
even come when their names are called. Oxen are better
than horses in rough terrain. Horses move faster than oxen
do, and work well when pulling a plow in a clean field, but
oxen are better at almost any task that requires steadi-

ness and patience rather than speed. Oxen are less susceptible to disease, adapt better to very warm and very cold climates, and are cheaper than horses in nearly every way. Usually, yokes of four or six oxen were used to pull the heavy wagons on the westward journey.

A few more days would bring us to the Green River crossing. The stream, while not very wide, was deep, and the stock would have to swim it and pull the wagons across. Remembering the ordeal of the Platte we anticipated this crossing with anxiety, although we did not expect the difficulties to be nearly so great.

When we arrived at the crossing our men began making preparations. First, they cut green saplings and sawed them into fourteen-inch lengths, four for each wagon. These timbers were placed upright on the bolsters and were fastened as securely as possible to the wagon standards. Then the boxes, or wagon beds, were set on these uprights and accordingly raised fourteen inches higher. In this position they were securely lashed with ropes. Thus it was planned to bring the supplies across without damage. The water was so deep, however, that it flowed into the elevated wagon boxes, wetting the lower layers.

Only the larger and stronger of the horses and oxen were thought to be adequate to draw the wagons through the deep water, and the animals were selected for this task. The remainder of the stock, including the other work stock with their harnesses, were forced to swim the river. This method required crossing and re-crossing for each laden wagon, and consumed much time, but it seemed the only way in which the crossing could be made. The boys of the wagon train again showed their courage and loyalty, for it was their task

*A nineteenth-century photograph captures a
typical frontier town scene: a wagon train
and its resting teams of oxen.*

to bring the stock across, and they were wet from
morning till night. There being no storms to interfere with our progress, such as we had at the Platte,
everything finally was brought across in safety.

So much of our goods got wet in crossing that it
took us another day to get them dried out. Even some
of our provisions got wet in the wagons and we had to
take care quickly to save them. But as soon as we
could, we resumed our journey unfalteringly.

Soon we were in a mountainous country where
we encountered some pretty steep climbs and equally steep descents. One of these places I remember
particularly because of the steepness. We had to dou-

ble up the teams and put the best wheel oxen to each wagon. At each stop for the winded animals, even with the brakes set to full strength and the men pushing the wagons, it was hard to keep them from rolling back down the grade. You may get some idea of the steepness and height of the mountain when I tell you that some of us, walking on ahead, reached the summit and on looking back could see no wagons. Everything below seemed enveloped in fog. When the wagons arrived we noticed that they were all wet, having been caught in a shower of rain while we, who were above the clouds, which we had mistaken for fog, had been in sunshine all the while.

We were not on the main trail, as I previously mentioned, having taken a cutoff to avoid the Salt Lake route with its scarcity of grass and water, intending to reach the Bear River Valley by way of Weber Canyon. After a hard journey we finally reached it, and found it a very interesting place, a small Mormon colony having settled in the valley a short time before.

10
A MORMON SETTLEMENT

The stream meandered through grassy stretches, vivid with beautiful flowers of varied hues. There was also considerable shrubbery and numerous large trees over which vines clambered like a network. At one place a cascade of perhaps a dozen rivulets descended from high up on the mountainside and broke over a rocky ledge in a perpendicular fall of perhaps four hundred feet, affording us a beautiful and inspiring sight of rare beauty.

MORMON IS THE NAME commonly used for members of the Church of Jesus Christ of Latter-day Saints. As they accept the Book of Mormon as holy scripture, they are often simply called Mormons. Joseph Smith, a modern prophet, published the Book of Mormon and founded the religion in 1830. In 1847, the Mormons, fleeing persecution because of their religious beliefs, left their homes in Illinois to follow the Oregon Trail to the valley of the Great Salt Lake in Utah. Their leader at this time was Brigham Young, who led an advance party of Mormon pioneers along the Green River and past Jim Bridger's establishment on Black's Fork and on to Salt Lake Valley. Bridger was a famous mountain man who spent most of his time trapping and exploring the Western wilderness.

Brigham Young's route was to become known as the Mormon Trail. It led almost directly west from Fort Kearny, Nebraska, to the Great Salt Lake. From the settlement at

Salt Lake City, Mormon satellite colonies were established throughout the territory. The first Mormon settlers planted crops of grain and vegetables for later migrations of Mormons from the East and from Europe who followed in wagons or on foot, pushing handcarts loaded with their belongings. After gold was discovered in California in 1848, thousands of gold rush fortune-seekers used the Mormon Trail.

In a short time, wherever they settled, the industrious and resourceful Mormon people built bridges and roads and made the desert bloom in a large-scale demonstration of what irrigation could do. Through the second half of the nineteenth century, the Mormons in Salt Lake Valley operated the only large farming ventures between the state of Colorado and the Pacific Coast.

*F*or several days we traveled down the Weber Canyon (as we then knew it), finding the road rough and rugged and not well defined. We zigzagged back and forth across the valley several times, crossing the stream flowing through it. The mountain scenery here was the most beautiful we had encountered.

After a long, rough journey we crossed the divide overlooking the Bear River Valley, still following the uneven road which showed but little travel, for it was only a local road used by the few Mormons coming from Salt Lake City to form the new settlement in this valley.

This valley was really some distance off our road, but we had been advised to come this way because of the abundance of feed and water on this little-used route. For the sake of our thin, tired stock, so badly in need of feed and rest, we thought it best to come this way. Few other trains ever traveled this route, preferring to keep to the main trail.

A period woodcut records the passage of a group of Mormons—men, women, and children—by foot to the Great Salt Lake in Utah. Their route became known as the Mormon Trail.

Having not heard of the Mormon settlement, we were somewhat disturbed to find them already in possession of the valley. But our fears were soon dissipated when we came into contact with these people, for they treated us kindly and welcomed us to the valley, saying there was plenty of room and feed for our animals.

Before reaching the valley proper we encountered an obstacle that caused us a great deal of trouble. This was the final descent into the valley. A flood from the melting snows had washed out the road ahead of us, leaving a sheer drop of eight or ten feet and, since there was no way round it, we had to take the wagons down that wall.

The men went to work with such tools as the train possessed, cutting brush and poles to fill in the huge ditch along with dirt and gravel. Even this material was hard to get with our crude tools; but they did the best they could to make the road passable. Still, at its best the road looked impassable for anything but foot travel. The steep pitch and the uneven surface afforded poor footing for the teams, and it seemed that the heavy wagons would crush everything before them as they rolled down the embankment.

The men unhitched all the horses from the wagons, and in their stead they placed the best wheel oxen of the train. Here Old Buck, the Platte River troublemaker and his mate came into good play, for they, being big and strong, were considered the best team to hold back the load. The wagons were rolled by hand as near to the embankment as was possible with safety. The oxen were hitched to the wagons, and ropes tied to the rear axles were held by the men in a mighty tug-of-war. Then began the perilous descent.

The oxen seemed to exercise almost super-intelligence in the way they handled themselves. They guided their footsteps, and held back with all their might. The men, holding the ropes, tugged with all their strength to keep the heavy wagons from speeding down the hillside.

One by one all the wagons reached the level ground below. This difficult task was accomplished without accident, although the slightest miscalculation might have had serious results. One entire day was spent getting the wagons down, the same team of oxen being used all the time, but they were unhitched occasionally and were allowed to feed and rest.

The boys in charge of the loose stock found a place where the banks were not so badly washed out, and they drove the animals down one at a time until all were safely brought into the valley. The women and children managed to scramble down by holding to vines and bushes growing in the crevices of the rocks.

Some of them formed a line and passed the babies from hand to hand until the level was reached. No stop was made for the noon meal, everyone ate a lunch "on the go." The descent was accomplished in time for us to prepare a good supper—a meal all were needing.

The next morning we were ready to start our journey again, and by two o'clock we arrived at the Mormon settlement, which was indeed a beautiful place. A clear, running stream crossed the valley, providing water to irrigate the gardens. The vegetables were just ready for use and we purchased some at a reasonable price, but many of the settlers gave us vegetables without charge. It had been months since we tasted fresh vegetables, and the memory of these crisp Mormon vegetables lingers with me yet.

The settlement was compactly built with green fields of grain in front of the houses, and flourishing vegetable gardens to the rear. The roadway passed between the fields and the houses. The Mormons told us they had built the community on this plan to afford protection from the Indians, for at that time the Mormons were encroaching on Indian lands. Sentries were posted and the people kept guard night and day.

The Mormon settlers were not expecting to see emigrant trains through this part of the country, and our coming caused quite a bit of excitement. Almost at once we were surrounded by settlers dressed in old-country clothes and wooden shoes. They were as much a curiosity to us as we were to them. They wanted to buy guns and ammunition from us, but we felt we could not spare any, for we were still in a part of the country where dangerous Indians roamed.

All the houses in the tiny community were built double, that is, two houses very much alike were built near each other with a passageway between. They were all newly built, mostly of logs. Some had adobe walls, and all had dirt-covered roofs and dirt floors. Wood was plentiful in the nearby mountains, but as yet there were no sawmills.

We heard afterwards of Indian uprisings against these people, but the settlement was able to protect itself. Its location was very desirable, and the colony grew and prospered.

We remained here talking with the settlers for three or four hours. We considered ourselves fortunate to find a friendly settlement where we could obtain all the nice vegetables we needed. As we left, they directed us to a good campsite four or five miles farther on, and told us we were welcome to use it and that there was plenty of water and good feed for the stock, but they warned us to be on the lookout for unfriendly Indians.

We had no Indian trouble in this part of the country. Grass and water now were plentiful and we traveled steadily along and soon reached the Bear River crossing. The water was low and we crossed without difficulty and continued on our way. Soon we came to a rough, broken country with scant grass and brackish water.

After a few days' travel we reached Soda Springs, our next landmark. It was a strong, clear-looking stream emerging from the ground and, the day being hot, we rushed thirstily with our cups to get a good, cool drink of water. But, ugh! what a taste it had. No one wanted a second cup, nor did we stay long. Instead, we looked for a more inviting place to camp.

11

CONTINUING ON THE TRAIL

Here, for a moment, let me digress to say that in recent years I have been over this same country, and found it far from being the desert it was when I first saw it. Irrigation has caused the change. Then, we called it the Great Sagebrush Desert. Today it is the Twin Falls and Minidoka tract. I beheld it with amazement and wonder. It has been transformed into a land of inviting homes, rich farm lands, and orchard tracts, the windswept waste has become an imperial domain. This is only one of the many wonderful and unbelievable changes wrought in the country since my coming in 1864.

THE FLATLAND known as the Great Plains was the last part of the Western frontier to be settled and farmed. There were many reasons why settlement was delayed. First, the region had a harsh climate with extremes of heat and cold, violent storms, and uncertain rainfall. Second, the absence of trees made it difficult to build or heat homes. The third reason was that the land was covered with tough grass, making it difficult to plow and seed. Fourth, the Indians of the Great Plains were fierce and warlike. For a long time this region was thought to be so unfit for settlement that it was nicknamed the "Great American Desert."

With the passage of the Homestead Act, tens of thousands of settlers poured into the region and learned to cope with its extraordinary difficulties. Periodically, settlers

Traveling over the Great Plains

were plagued by grasshoppers in swarms so thick they stopped trains and gobbled up everything they could chew. The settlers also endured droughts so severe that cattle and crops perished and the thin topsoil blew away in giant duststorms. Some early settlers left the region in despair, but thousands came in to replace them.

Miners, lured to the Great Plains-Rocky Mountains region by the news of gold and silver strikes, also helped to settle the territory. Oddly many of the miners who came to the region were prospectors from California. When the gold deposits there had been mined out, California gold seekers began working their way back east. When the gold and silver eventually played out in this region, too, many miners remained in the mining camps that became new towns. The miners provided the farmers in the region with a ready-made market for their crops of grain and vegetables.

*F*ort Hall was our next point of interest. We reached it without mishap, but had to travel over a long stretch of uninviting country before we arrived. Some of our companions had decided to go on to California, and Fort Hall would be our parting place. The family suffering the tragedy at the Platte were also leaving at this point. The mother had never wholly recovered from the shock, but seemed always sad and depressed and showed no interest in anything around her, not even in the care of her small children.

The daughter, however, had become her normal self again. She was devoted to her mother and was patient in her care of her small brothers and sister. The young man who drove their wagon seemed fond of her and we all hoped the interest was mutual and would lead to their marriage. The mother and the small children were so lonely and helpless and so much in need of someone to protect them and look after their welfare that the young man's interest seemed like a godsend.

Our next point of interest was the Snake River crossing. This, we learned, would be somewhere near the mouth of the Blackfoot River, and we would cross on a ferry which was operated mainly for the benefit of the soldiers at Fort Hall.

The journey from Fort Hall to the Snake River was uneventful. The country was mostly a sagebrush desert, from level to rolling. We made an easy crossing of the Snake River on the ferry, and though we were eager to see this river, our eagerness to continue our journey prevented any delay, and we contented ourselves with observing it as we crossed. Each mile gained now brought us nearer our destination.

A long, tedious strip of desert now lay ahead of us, and the going was rough and tiresome. Beds of burned lava rock cut the feet of the cattle and made them limp, and the wagons bumped along noisily and crunched the cinders in the road. The cattle became so lame they could hardly travel, and when we reached better ground, we had to give them several days' rest before we could proceed.

Water was extremely short in this desert, and grazing was wholly inadequate for the needs of the stock. When the captain at last informed us that we were now leaving the desert and would strike across a low range of hills to the Lost River country, we were much encouraged. We were eager to make the change. We hoped also to find the scenery less monotonous and more cheerful. The long desert journey had taken toll of our good spirits.

We had by this time lost all fear of being molested by Indians, having not seen any since entering the great desert country. Our hunters said not even jack rabbits could subsist in that country, much less Indians and their ponies. The danger eliminated, more freedom was permitted the stock in grazing, for as yet, because of the immigration ahead of us, our stock had to be taken some distance from the train for feed.

The long rest and relaxation made us feel better, and the delightful change in the topography of the country tended to raise our spirits. Our stock was refreshed and filled up and seemed contented for the first time in weeks; so the next morning we started on with lighter hearts.

We were now skirting some high, rough-looking

mountains, and occasionally had to climb some steep hills. We crossed innumerable mountain streams of pure, fresh water, some of them being so large as to be impassable in high water season. But this was low water season and we made all crossings without much trouble. At times, however, we put the best teams to the wheel, in event we came to swimming water. Old Buck, then, because of his sturdy qualities was brought into use, he and his mate, faithful old brutes that they were.

The rivers and streams were the landmarks by which we measured distance and estimated our progress, but I have forgotten many of their names. I remember the Wood River and the delightful camping spot it afforded us; also the washing and clean up with which the women kept up their habits of cleanliness on every practicable occasion was remarkable. We found so many nice, clear streams of soft water that the men complained about so much washing, saying the women were forever wanting to stop and wash. They argued that, since we traveled in dust, cooked and ate in dust, slept in dust and dirt, and were in it all the time, why should we go to the trouble of washing and cleaning so often?

It did seem futile, and we could not give a good reason for so much washing, except that it was a habit and a desire to see the children clean, and to feel clean ourselves once in a while. Further, we said, we were not stopping any too often for the good of the stock. This last argument was a clincher. Our whole dependence was on our animals, and some of them were getting very thin, worn, and weary, and so much in need of rest.

Though compelled to travel slowly, we were making pretty good progress and were now nearing Big Camas Prairie where we hoped to find a plentiful supply of grass for the stock, having heard favorable reports from that part of the country. But alas! The country had been invaded by a horde of crickets, which had eaten every blade of grass in sight! The grass had grown rank and tall, but the stems were standing devoid of blades and were covered with dozens of big, brown, ugly-looking insects. This would have been a glorious place for Indian harvest, for they were said to gather these crickets for food; but no Indians were in evidence. There were so many small streams of good water, and so many nice level spots suitable for camping, that, had the grass been plentiful, we could have found ideal stopping places. But we pushed on as rapidly as possible in order to find good grass, and we didn't even stop for noon lunch. After a drive of several miles we found a little stream the crickets had not reached, and here in the midst of good feed for our stock, we made our camp.

We had met several prospectors along the streams, and once had met a small pack train going to Fort Hall for supplies. The mountains, we were informed, were full of prospectors, drawn to this region by the discovery of rich mines at Bannock the year before. Thinking we were making for the mines, our informants advised us not to go there this fall, saying that the snow would soon fall and would get so deep in the winter that no mining could be done.

They were astonished when we told them we had not heard about the strike, but were on our way to Oregon, for they imagined the news had spread everywhere. They told us all about the great gold rush. The rich discovery had been made in 1862, but was kept quiet. By '63, however, it had become pretty well-noised around, and a great rush, mostly from the West, had occurred. Many old Forty-niners from California were in the camp. The excitement was so great throughout the West, they said, that they could not understand how we had failed to hear about it. We explained that perhaps the Civil War, which was

Prospecting for gold

the absorbing topic where we came from, had over-shadowed the news; and anyway, reports had to travel very slowly to reach the East. Our story of the War was nearly as much news to the prospectors as the gold strike was to us. They didn't seem to realize there was a war; at least they were not concerned about it. Their concern was in the gold find. Our concern now was to get to Oregon before the snow caught us on this side of the Cascade Mountains.

From now on we became conscious of a stir of life and activity in the country. We began to meet people going and coming, and once we overtook an emigrant train of a few wagons. They also had gathered the news of the gold mines, and of far greater interest to us, of the fine valley we would shortly reach and of the settlement being made there.

12

FORT BOISE

*I little thought, as we crossed the ferry that
September day and landed on the Boise side of
the river, that my long journey had reached its
end. But it had, and ten wonderful years of my
life were to be spent in Boise Valley.*

FORT BOISE was built by the Hudson Bay Company in
1834 as a fur-trading outpost. The name Boise comes from
the French word bois, which means wooded. Unlike the
dry, treeless region of the Snake River plains to the east,
Boise is situated where trees are plentiful, as they are
watered by melting snow from the mountains. The climate
is dry overall, with some areas desertlike. The settlement
was on the bank of the Boise River, a tributary of the Snake
River, and settlers used both as water supplies. During the
summer the weather is warm, and the winters are cold with
snowstorms not uncommon. Still, miners and farmers came
here to mine for gold and silver or to start farms. By 1863,
enough people had moved to Idaho for it to become a territory. There were 25,000 people in the Boise area alone.

One day we met a man with a load of fresh vegetables. He said he was from the Boise Valley
about thirty miles farther on. He had raised the veg-

etables there, he told us, and knowing the emigrants were starving for fresh vegetables, he had decided to come out and meet us with a load. In this he had judged rightly, for we were very, very hungry for the vegetables, having not tasted any since leaving the Bear River Valley several weeks before.

But here we found ourselves in a dilemma. As you know, during the Civil War our government, being at times hard-pressed for money acceptable to foreign countries, had withdrawn from circulation all gold and silver money and had substituted paper money called greenbacks. For small change, less than a dollar, it had issued small paper slips commonly called shinplasters, in denominations ranging in value from five cents up. So far, we had met with no difficulty in passing them for money. The French-Canadian post traders along the way had accepted them gladly in payment for the purchases we had acquired. Lately, however, having reached the western borders where there was but little trade with the East, this small paper money was completely ignored. The people said they could not use them at all. They accepted our greenbacks, however, at a 50 percent discount.

Now, we wanted so much to buy some of those luscious vegetables, and the settler wanted just as much to sell them. But all we had to offer him were those little shinplasters, and he said he could not use them at all. He said he would accept our greenbacks down to one dollar denominations, but at a 50 percent discount. A greenback dollar at that rate would not buy many vegetables; furthermore, our money was so scarce we could not afford to spend it in this manner. Though we were anxious to get rid of our shinplasters, even at a discount, we could buy only with our depreciated greenbacks. Ruinous business, but nevertheless we did buy some of his vegetables, and how delicious they tasted!

A new settlement in the Northwest

That night we camped in a nice little ravine, the settler with his vegetables stopping near us. The next morning he let us have the rest of his vegetables very reasonably, for he knew they would soon become stale. We tried again to induce him to accept some of our shinplasters, but he said no, they would do him no good. He couldn't dispose of them. He didn't know that the laws of the country compelled their acceptance as legal tender. The East and West were so remote, both in distance and in relation, that the national law of legal tender was not recognized in the West. Out of the goodness of his heart the peddler gave vegetables without charge to those who offered him shinplasters, thinking, perhaps, that they had no other money. Then he hurried off ahead of us with his empty wagon.

After traveling a few miles up the canyon we came out on a high plateau of level land covered with the usual growth of sagebrush. By this time we had seen so much sagebrush that we all detested the smell as well as the sight of it, and on this high bench of land stretching between the Boise River and the Snake River far to the south of us, we beheld sagebrush as far as the eye could see! A veritable ocean of sagebrush! We were told that we could find water about fifteen miles farther on, so we traveled that day without nooning and camped earlier in the evening.

The next morning we discovered that a horse belonging to my brother-in-law had become lame and was unable to travel. Several members of the train said they would go on to the Boise Valley and find a good camping ground and wait for us there. A number of wagons belonging to our party stayed with us; those who were related made a point of staying together. Our camping place was not so nice and shady as we would have liked it, but it was not a lonely place, for there were occasional passers-by who stopped to chat with us, telling us all about the wonderful mines recently found, and giving us a full account of the settlement in the Boise Valley and all the news relative to it. Another man came by with vegetables and we purchased some, but he, like the others, refused to accept our little paper money in payment.

That night another train came along and camped with us, and as we had many new things to tell them, we had a lively camp. In return they gave us news of some of the members of our train who had been left behind to recover their loose cattle. Among other things they told us the sorrowful news of a little four-year-old girl who had fallen out of the wagon and had been run over and killed. She was buried by the roadside, and her mother was broken-hearted at having to leave her little darling sleeping in that vast, lonely solitude where even the consolation of visiting her grave was forever denied the grief-stricken mother. We had counted many such graves on that long trail. Some were marked by a rock or rude headstone with faded inscription. Often only a stake driven into the ground marked the burial spot.

We remained in this camp three days, during which time all the horses were newly shod. After the rest and long grazing period they were able to travel better. An early morning start enabled us to make it across to the Boise River where we camped for the night. The horse's leg was still pretty stiff and sore, but at the end of the day it seemed no worse for the travel.

The next morning we broke camp, traveled down the river five or six miles, and crossed on a ferry boat. Many others of our party kept on down the south side of the river until they reached a place where they could ford it. The water at that time was very low, but even at that there was some danger to be incurred in crossing, for the river was wide and swift. The risk was taken principally because of the low financial condition of the train, and our reluctance to part with our United States currency at the exorbitant discount in vogue here. This, and the absolute refusal of the settlers to accept our shinplasters, worked a hardship on all of us.

Our reason for crossing on the ferry was to see the little town of Boise, which was just starting up. The men also wanted to verify some of the reports they had heard about the mines.

The town of Boise was a little, motley collection of log cabins, tents, and dugouts. There were perhaps

The dry air of the elevated plateau west of the Mississippi caused wood to shrink. Thus, most evenings, the wagon-train blacksmith was busy repairing buckets, wheels, and other equipment, along with shoeing horses and mules.

two or three rude frame buildings, not very symmetrical in appearance, for axes and saws had been the principal tools used in their construction. The lumber came from a little sawmill up in the Bannock Mountains. The mill had been brought in with great difficulty on pack horses, over trails too steep for wagons. Lumber, however, was a necessity for making sluice boxes and flumes for washing the gold from the mines. Bringing the lumber from the mill to the town was also very difficult. I believe only three houses in the town were built of lumber, these being the main eating house, dignified by the name hotel, one small store, and a very pretentious saloon and dance hall.

Crude and primitive as it was then, I little thought it the embryo of one of the prettiest and finest little cities I have ever seen in all my travels, as it appeared to me in 1927 when it was my good fortune to spend a week with some of its hospitable people, after an absence of fifty years. At the time of my visit to Boise in 1927, sixty-three years had elapsed since I first saw the little town on September 25, 1864. My pen cannot adequately describe the changes wrought in building up and beautifying the city. Green, velvety lawns, beautiful flowers, well-laid parks, lovely homes, fine business edifices, lakes and bathing pools, parks containing wild animals, schools, churches, and other improvements too numerous to mention, now bespeak the civic pride of her citizenry. How different from the Boise I first knew!

I found only one person—an old lady—who was my fellow traveler on that memorable journey still living here, although quite a number of my own train stopped here and became residents of Boise.

How we happened to stay here, and how we built up a home in this new country, is related in the pages immediately following.

13

BOISE CAMPSITE

The first little looking glass was the source of many good natured jokes that first winter, and for years afterwards it was a cherished piece of furnishing in our home, long after we were able to get a better glass. We kept it all the years we lived in the Boise Valley.

WHEN THEY ARRIVED in Boise, Frank Fulton, a local farmer and freight hauler, brought melons and vegetables to people in Arabella's wagon train. Grateful members of the wagon train invited Frank to share Sunday dinner with them. During the evening, Frank offered Arabella's brother-in-law, Jimmie Purdin, a job for the winter. The job paid fifty dollars a month and came with room and board for Jimmie and his wife, Angie, who would do the cooking and housekeeping. Arabella was to come too, since she was part of the family. The third sister, Addie, and her husband, Tom Jones, made similar arrangements with a neighbor of Frank's.

With money running low and uncertain of getting work at the end of the journey, Jimmie accepted Frank's offer. Planning to move on, with his wife and Arabella, after he had saved up enough money, he agreed to help build the Fulton house. Until it was completed, however, all four adults were to live in a makeshift camp.

Hugh Allen, Frank's business partner and best friend, lived with the group from time to time.

Mr. Fulton informed my brother-in-law that the first work to be done was a job of carpentry, laying the foundations for a house he was preparing to build. He had the logs already hewed and squared up for a one-and-a-half-story house, and had some boards rived out for a roof. He said we would have to live in a camp until he could get the house built. Then he added, "Perhaps you'd better fix up camp a little handier, and go to town one day soon and get what is needed. Our camp is very scant."

Jimmie said we would wait a few days more before going to town, and take a look over things to see what we most needed. Mr. Fulton replied that he was very busy himself, and could not be around camp much. He wanted to make two more trips to the mines, and must start as soon as the oxen were found.

He was hauling to the mines some hay he had baled with a home-made baler, and some oats he had raised and threshed out with oxen trampling out the grain, biblical style, and separated from the chaff with a hand-operated fanning mill he had rented from someone who had brought it into the valley that fall. The crop had been raised by means of irrigation, and ditches had been made to convey the water from the river to the land.

These commodities were very scarce, and precious, but he received a good price for his hay and oats when he got them to market—one hundred fifty dollars a ton for the hay, and fifteen cents a pound for the oats. He would have received a fabulous price for his vegetables, but he said he could not spare them, now that he had someone to cook them.

Mr. Fulton told Jimmie to take an inventory of the provisions he had left in the wagon, and he would pay him the going price for them. We had several

A wagon train arrives at Boise City.

pounds of good, fat bacon sides, and I think one sack of flour, which at that time was worth seven dollars a sack. Bacon was fifty cents a pound. The smaller quantities of stuff, Jimmie said, we would eat in common.

We really needed some camp fixtures, and my sister wanted to do some purchasing, and as Mr. Fulton needed some bolts to repair the wagon brakes, we decided to go to town, a fifteen-mile drive in a heavy wagon, to do a very little bit of buying.

The next morning, as we were getting ready to go

to town, the "old bachelor," as my sister and I called him by ourselves, came down. (He objected to being called Mr. Fulton, saying the mister was too formal and that no one used the term here. I had noticed that they used only the surname. He wanted us to call him Frank, but Addie and I could not bring ourselves to be so familiar. However, Jimmie came to it very easily, and in course of time, we came to it, too. It seemed to please him; he said that was more like friends.) He handed me a little sack of gold dust, saying "Here is ten dollars. I thought you might want to buy something you need."

"Oh, no!" I replied, "I don't want your money."

"I thought you might want to buy something for the camp," he said. Thereupon, I told him I would take it if he would tell me what he wanted me to buy.

"You women all know better than I what you need about camp," he replied.

I knew what I wanted to buy. We had no looking glass in camp, and Oh, how I did miss one!

When I got to town it was the first thing I began to look for. I found one, about ten by twelve inches, frame and all, and paid three dollars for it! Then I bought a comb and some towels. I begged an empty cigar box for a comb holder, bought a washboard and tub, and found my money about all spent.

It was getting late that evening when we reached home, but I had Jimmie hasten to drive a nail in a tree and nail up the box for the comb. The towel was hung nearby.

"I shall try to make this place more homelike, so you men won't go down to the creek and wash in that cold water," I said. Oh, yes! I had bought a washpan also, and we hung it up on the tree. Then we appropriated one of the benches for a washstand.

When Mr. Fulton came to supper, I saw him note the change. He cast his eye on the looking glass and I saw a broad smile come over his face. I knew he wanted to say something funny, but was a little afraid to do it. When Jimmie came in he soon opened the way. It all turned on a woman's proverbial liking for a looking glass. Jimmie was a good match for Mr. Fulton, or rather, Mr. Fulton made a good mate for Jimmie, who was always a great joker. It usually was I who had to bear the brunt of Jimmie's jokes, for his wife wouldn't stand for them.

I let the two men enjoy their jokes and laugh as much as they liked. But after supper I said: "Now, I hope you will digest your dinner better; but I know I will not be the only one who will use that glass. I expect to see someone shaving before many days."

Frank, or rather Mr. Fulton, I should say, had a long, full beard which looked as if it had not known a razor for some time. While it was common for men to wear full beards, usually they shaved off their moustaches when they dressed up for Sunday. Jimmie knew he just had to shave, for his wife made him.

On the road we had used my other sister's little glass, and we all had our combs. The men, I presume, had theirs also, but doubtless they were getting old and needed to be replaced with new ones. However, I evened up with them when they went to use my glass for shaving. I demanded an insurance that their looks would not break it every time they used it.

14
FULTON HOUSE

Mr. Fulton had made arrangements, though, to get some lumber for finishing the house, for the fall rains might set in and find us still in camp without much shelter.

THE REAL FRONTIER STORY is the story of plain people struggling for land, building homes, and raising families in a hard, unsettled land. The pioneer family's first shelter was either a "soddy"—a sod-covered dugout, often cut into a hillside—or a tiny wood cabin. More often than not, these structures were infested with snakes, mice, and bedbugs, making life miserable for the human occupants.

People living in wild country away from others were inventive and independent. Any advantage one person had over another was based solely on ability. The harder you worked the more you could acquire. Pioneers also had a strong faith in the future. Most pioneers felt that things would get better over time.

Arabella Clemens Fulton's life serves as a good example of the pioneers' faith in the future. The construction of the cabin that would become her first home as a married woman remained a vivid and happy memory all her life. This farm woman carefully cultivated the pioneer spirit in the minds of her children so that today even her grand-

children and their children know where the original homestead cabin stood.

*F*inally the house was ready to put up, and several
men came to help with the raising. We had to
cook dinner on a campfire for all of them. Mr. Fulton
always relished getting off a joke on me. On the morning they were preparing to lay the foundation for the
house, he came down to camp in a great hurry, as
though he were after something very important, and
said to me: "We are ready to lay the foundation of the
house now, and you'd better come tell us where you
want to place it."

I was somewhat taken aback at this proposition,
but I replied: "Oh, it's nothing to me where you put
your house. Just put it wherever you like."

"I thought you might have a choice later on," he
answered.

"No, I think not," I replied.

This gave Jimmie another chance to tease me.

They got the logs set up that day, and Mr. Fulton
left the men to cover the house and make the chimney
while he made a trip to get lumber for the floors and
doors.

The rafters were made of poles smoothed off on
one side, and the sheeting was of split poles, notched
and made to fit the rafters. The roofing shakes were
three feet long. The lower part of the chimney was
made of split poles, built together on the same plan as
the house, about five feet square, and with only three
sides. The ends of the poles forming the three-sided
square, if there be such a figure, were fitted between
the logs of the house where a space of about three
feet was sawed out in order to attach the chimney to
the house. The inside of this frame was faced with

A sod-covered hut, often the first home for prairie settlers

mud and cobblestones to a thickness of ten or twelve inches. This facing was called the back and jamb of the chimney.

All this consumed a lot of time, and the weather was threatening rain, so they hired another man, who claimed to be an expert, to build the chimney. He said he knew how to shape it so that it would not smoke in the house. Hugh [Frank's partner and business associate] and Jimmie didn't know a thing in the world about chimneys, and were glad to turn the job over to him. But the chimney was the bane of our lives. When the wind blew from the east it always smoked us out. Being of "stick-and-dirt" construction, it didn't stand the elements very well either, and the mud would crack and fall out occasionally.

A heavy snow storm caught Frank while he was in the mountains after his lumber and he had a hard time getting back, being three days overdue, at that, he could bring only half of it. The next spring when he went back after the rest he found someone else had taken it. He had traded for two cows from an emigrant going to the mines that fall, and tried to bring them home tied behind his wagon; one cow gave out, and the other was so thin and weak when he arrived that we could not feed her up sufficiently to withstand the rigors of the hard winter and she died.

However, she left a little calf, which was given to me, and this was the nucleus of the nice dairy herd I had when we sold out ten years later to go to Texas. The mother had lived until the calf was about three weeks old and had given a little milk for it. After that we ground corn on a hand mill and made gruel for it. Sometimes we would spare a little of our precious flour for mixing the gruel, and again, I would boil wild hay and make the calf a tea to drink. I was very proud of my ability to save it, and indeed, it was my very own and not a partnership calf! It thrived and grew, and became an extraordinarily good milk cow.

When he got back with his lumber, Mr. Fulton, or Frank, as we were now calling him, was tired and worn out for want of sleep and from floundering around in the snow, unloading and reloading his lumber so often on account of the storm and bad roads. He was much relieved when he reached the valley to find that we had not had a hard rain.

"Now," he said, "we must hurry up with the house." He thought himself fortunate to get one small window with four panes of glass, which someone had ordered but had not been able to pay for. I have forgotten the price he had to pay for it, but it was high.

The architectural design of the house had not included a window, and this necessitated cutting out a space for it. They also cut a square hole in the door, covering it over with white cloth to give additional light when the door had to be closed in cold weather. Most doors stood open when the weather would permit, this being the only means of lighting. Ours would be a window to the good of the other houses in the valley.

15
GETTING MARRIED

I had now given up my name — that of my father and my family, a name in which I had always taken a high and conscious pride, the name of Clemens.

THE WESTERN HOMESTEADER was isolated from civilization, but for exactly that reason the homesteading man needed a wife, and the survival of the pioneer woman often depended on her acquisition of a husband. Every day brought a grinding succession of the most primitive chores and unless the work was shared, prosperity would remain out of reach. This human need for a helpmate, plus desire for companionship, brought Arabella Clemens and Frank Fulton together.

What did pioneer men and women look for in choosing their mates? Certainly, a young man who did not want to work hard and become prosperous was not likely to be chosen. A young woman who was thrifty, hardworking, respectable, and available would undoubtedly be married quickly. Arabella brought to the marriage other desirable qualities: she had good general health and a confidence that she and Frank, working together, would be able to meet life's challenges.

*F*rank came to me one day and said: "I would like to have a little private talk with you if you will give me a chance."

I did not look up nor answer, but kept my eyes pretty steady on my potato peeling.

"I presume you know what I want to talk about," he said.

"No, I haven't the least idea," I replied. He knew I was fibbing.

"Well," he said, "I can soon tell you if you will give me a chance."

Then I looked up at him and said: "You see we haven't a very convenient chance here."

"If you will come and sit by the campfire this evening, I can soon tell you what I am thinking, and give you a chance to say something."

"All right," I told him. "I will sit awhile with you after supper." He thanked me and went away.

I was quite a bit flustered that night while getting supper ready—and who wouldn't have been? In my own mind I knew I was not going to reject him; and yet, I knew full well that I was not well enough acquainted with him to marry him and put myself in his keeping. Fortunately for both of us, he was very considerate about the matter, soon putting me at ease as we sat by the campfire that night.

"I am not asking you to pledge yourself," he said, "or to give me your answer now. I am only wanting at this time to tell you my desire and give you a chance to think the matter over while I am gone on this trip. You know I need a wife, and I cannot make a home without one. You suit me, and you are just the one I want."

I smiled a little, perhaps encouragingly, and said: "Why, you don't know me yet. We are not well enough

The emigrants' experience, as recorded by an artist of the time. Top: "On the Road." Center: "Crossing a River." Bottom right: "The First Season." Bottom left: "The Second Season."

acquainted to know whether we would suit each other."

To this he answered: "No, you have no chance to know me, and you have the right to feel that way about it. My rough garb, rough manners, and rough surroundings are all against me. For this reason, I want to give you time to study over the matter. "As for myself," he continued, "I am very willing to take you as I find you. I have observed you more closely than you knew. I have seen you gathering the seeds from the garden and putting them away carefully, and keeping the work done about the camp so nicely, and appearing so willing in every way to do your part. I know you better than you know me."

"Well," I replied, "I wanted to do something to pay for my board. You know you and Jimmie wouldn't let me take that job at the hotel, which would have paid me sixty dollars a month. It was Jimmie, of course who did the objecting, but I thought perhaps you were back of him."

Disregarding the suggestion of Jimmie's being the principal, "No," he cried, "I couldn't let you go there. It is too rough a place for any good girl to work."

I told him I thought I was able to take care of myself, but nevertheless, I thanked him for his generous interest in not letting me take the position. Then I added, touching another phase: "I know you thought I was wasteful when I so freely cooked up all that bacon for which you paid Jimmie a good price. I know now that it should have lasted twice as long, but I was intent only on seasoning well and making the cooking more tasteful. I have always been accustomed to using plenty of bacon in cooking. Jimmie spoke to me about it. Perhaps you were behind him in that, too."

"No," he remonstrated, "I did not say anything about that, but," a little ruefully, "I could see that it was going pretty fast."

110

"Well, I am sorry I was so wasteful, but I will do better next time," I promised.

This was the place and the manner in which I received the proposal of marriage—not my first, however, I must have you know.

Frank did not get away on his trip for three or four days, and we had several more chats.

The house was now nearing completion, and it was about ready for us to move into. Its furnishings were the rudest, home-made furniture, which was the best we had. We cooked on a fireplace instead of a range, and our cooking utensils were pots and pans, and we ate from the dishes. My sister was in a delicate condition, and the one chair we possessed was reserved for her. Our tablecloth was a piece of oil-cloth, worn and soiled from hard usage on the Trail. A ladder led to the room above, where Hugh slept during bad weather. Bed "ticks" filled with wild hay answered for mattresses.

Addie brought her feather bed along, but there was not room to bring mine. We had brought some pillows, sheets, quilts, and home-made blankets, and the men had a plentiful supply of fine-quality, Oregon-made wool blankets. Since the downstairs part of the house consisted of only one big room, bedrooms were partitioned off with blankets, and the rest of the space served as a sitting room, dining room, and kitchen combined.

We were now ensconced in our new home. Rough, crude, and primitive though it was, it sheltered us from the storms of approaching winter. Jimmie and Hugh busied themselves making stables and shelter for the stock, and providing wood for winter fires.

After a fine rain, the weather turned a little warmer, and they decided to do some plowing. Jimmie hitched up the team and plowed about two acres near the house, which he laughingly told me was for my garden. In this he spoke more truly than he knew,

111

for in reality it became my garden spot the next spring, and I did wonders with that little garden. Plowing was continued until the third day of December, when the temperature took a sudden drop and a cold storm set in. The plow was left frozen in the ground.

The storm caught Frank in the Weiser River Valley on his return trip. Because of the threatening weather he had gone only to the Grand Ronde Valley in Oregon and bought his supplies there, and thus avoided crossing the Blue Mountains. A neighbor, Mr. Schooler, who went with him for supplies, went on to Umatilla Landing, but on account of the snow, was unable to return until late the next spring. We supplied his family from Frank's stock of goods. Had Frank not used better judgement than our neighbor, we all would have suffered for lack of food that winter. As it was, our flour was all consumed before Mr. Schooler arrived in the spring and we had bought two extra sacks from a packer at fifteen dollars a sack.

Though he cut his trip short by getting his supplies at Grand Ronde, Frank had a hard, difficult journey. The storm had come with heavy winds, then rain which, as it turned colder, turned to snow. He was fortunate, however, in finding sheltered places for camping and plenty of wood for fires. He made the return trip in three weeks. We were all much relieved and rejoiced to see him drive in. He appeared very worn and tired, but said he had suffered no harm from exposure, and he had kept well during the journey. His team was badly fagged and run down from the long, hard trip.

I think I gave him great pleasure by welcoming him warmly, and showing him I had not lost faith in him.

There was not much to do toward getting ready, as

I did not intend to get a wedding trousseau for the occasion, but to wear a dress I had brought with me.

The wedding dinner was a very plain affair. We had no eggs, nor was there any butter to be had, except the firkin butter made in New York and carried by ships around the Horn and on up the Pacific Coast to San Francisco or Portland, thence by pack train to the mines. It was by no means delicate when it arrived; the long ocean voyage had given it strength! The miners had become accustomed to it, but we tender-feet didn't relish it. We still had a few pumpkins from the garden, but no other ingredients for making pies. We made some pies, however, from the dried apples Frank had brought in with the winter supplies during the big storm. We also had rice, which in those days was considered a delicacy. For sweetening we had only brown sugar. We had some nice lard, so we made cookies instead of cake for the wedding. We managed to get a nice roast of mutton from a man who had brought in some sheep for the mines.

Our pies and cookies were baked in the Dutch ovens used on the Trail, and in skillets set on live coals drawn from the hearth. A hot iron lid covered with live coals was placed over the baking. We could make pies and cakes in this manner, but it was much more trouble than cooking in a stove. We also baked good salt-rising light bread in this way. Yeast was not available.

The next morning Jimmie went into the tent with Frank and did some barbering for him, and also for Hugh, and that was the last we saw of them that morning. My sister and I busied ourselves getting the dinner ready and furnishing other details. We expected the minister about twelve o'clock, and we wanted to have everything in readiness.

In due time the preacher arrived, and the men came into the house. This was the first time I had ever seen the man I was to marry shaved and neatly trimmed, and wearing a dress suit!

I was thrilled with pride! He was a fine-looking man, and his new suit fitted him admirably, setting off his well-made form to good advantage. Hitherto, I had always seen him in work clothes which, as such things go, were neat enough. I had never thought much about his appearance, admiring him more for his fine character and generous heart than for his good looks.

Now I had a new admiration for him. These thoughts had so engrossed me that I was completely absorbed in my admiration for him, and when they asked me if I was ready for the ceremony, it was so far removed from my mind that I was abashed, but I soon rallied from my abstraction and answered, "Yes, I am ready!"

When the ceremony was over we received the congratulations of my sister, my brother-in-law, and Hugh Allen. Hugh looked fine in his new suit, too. It was the first time I had seen him dressed up. The three signed their names to the Marriage Certificate, and the preacher said he would have it recorded if he ever got to a place where he could have it done. But I doubt if he ever did.

We then hastened with the dinner, for the preacher had a long way to return home that afternoon. The white tablecloth and the white dishes made the table look very attractive. The preacher said it was the best dinner he had eaten for a long time. You may know that we in this snow-bound valley were living on the barest necessities. But withal these crude surroundings, that was the happiest day of my life.

It was the twenty-fourth day of November, 1864.

16
A HOME IN THE WILDERNESS

I have given some of the details of that harrowing, unforgettable winter, but I couldn't begin to tell it all. Many people were too proud to let their wants be known, and kept their suffering and privations to themselves. However, this was our last winter of scarcity and suffering.

THE FIRST FULL YEAR was one of privation and suffering for Arabella and Frank. Most of the early pioneers found that the "land of opportunity" was in reality a place where they faced a quiet struggle to stay alive. Season after season, the early settlers led a difficult existence, enduring bitterly cold winters, fiercely hot summers, the starvation of their livestock, and their own constant hunger. Loneliness, and the dread of illness and childbirth in a land where professional medical help was either far away or nonexistent, added to their troubles. In addition, homesteading farmers had to tame the land from the start, and do it without the use of power equipment.

Cornmeal, sourdough, beef, tallow, some mutton, and any wild game they could shoot were common food staples. Gunnysacks were cut up for men's pants, children's clothes, and footwear. Women made do with one or two dresses and a winter shawl.

115

Soon winter set in in earnest, with a storm lasting several days. Then men killed the beef steer Frank had bought from his friend, Mr. Naylor, who had driven up a bunch of steers from southern Oregon for the mines. He had the animal before we came, but had delayed butchering it till cold weather, in order to keep the meat frozen. We let our neighbors, the Schoolers, have one quarter. All the fat and tallow we saved very carefully for cooking purposes. I can say truthfully that I got very tired of beef and tallow that winter, and yet we were fortunate, and thankful to have even this, for so many of our neighbors had none.

After the winter turned so cold I was unable any longer to make my salt-rising bread, and I had to learn the bachelor method of making sourdough biscuits. Having to turn them in beef tallow instead of lard made me lose my relish for them before many weeks had passed. We had buried some cabbage, rutabagas, and turnips in a pit to keep them from freezing, and these we considered a godsend. A few potatoes had also been "holed up," but were kept religiously for spring planting. Frank had raised all these in his garden that summer.

Seeds of all kinds were scarce. I had scrupulously gathered every seed I could from the garden that fall, and I saved them carefully. No seeds were to be had from the stores, and none were sent through the mail. Indeed, we had no certain mail then. Mrs. Naylor, in southern Oregon, had sent Frank most of the seeds he had planted in his garden, when Mr. Naylor had come over with the beef herd.

Once, while packing freight over the Blue Mountains, Frank had found a little pile of white beans, apparently spilled from a hole in a sack. These he

Farming on the prairie

had carefully picked up and planted in his garden. When our train arrived the beans were just right for cooking, and being tender and meaty, were most delicious. We named them the Blue Mountain Beans. I kept their seed in my family for many years, and when any of my children married and started homes of their own, I always gave them a planting of the Blue Mountain Beans, together with their history.

Frank also planted some yellow corn, bought for horse feed while packing, and from it he had harvested about forty bushels. It had been planted a little too late to mature well, but it proved a blessing to many people who were short of food that winter.

I had often expressed a desire for some corn bread, for I did not relish biscuits with vegetables; so, Frank, on one of his trips for supplies that fall, happened to find a little hand grinder, such as the Hudson Bay Company shipped in for sale to the Indians, and he purchased it. When he gave it to me, he said laughingly that he had bought it instead of a wedding ring. I thanked him for it and told him I thought it would be the more useful of the two, and so it proved to be before that long, cold, and dreary winter ended.

Let me here speak more words about that terrible winter. A band of sheep had been brought in for the miners. Some had been sold for mutton, but the owner still had about three hundred on hand when winter set in. One night a severe snow storm came up and completely covered the sheep as they stood bunched up or lay huddled together. Before spring more than half the remaining sheep died for lack of feed. This was a calamity, for not only for the owner, but for the settlers as well, for the flock would have provided mutton for a large number of them, and the owner would in time have been remunerated for his sheep.

Most of the wild game had been killed off or driven away by the emigrants. Some fish could be taken from the river, but the run this season was mostly what is called dog salmon, a very poor species, unfit for food. Yet, one of our neighbors, on earlier arrival, had packed a barrel of it in salt and in the lack of other food, said it was very good eating. This neighbor had also bought a few sacks of corn, and made cornmeal with a big coffee mill. Next spring, in telling us how his family managed to survive, he said: "We had five children, but I managed to keep them from starving or getting very hungry. They have worn out their shoes, but still they have stockings. My wife makes them moccasins out of old sacks, or anything she has. My two cows gave milk till the snow set in. I had managed to put up a little hay, which kept them from starving." He said they had a large side of bacon when they stopped here, which had helped tide them over the winter. He had brought, all the way from Iowa, six hens and one rooster, and these he had fed through the winter, dividing with them his scanty food supply.

Spring is advancing. Days are getting longer and warmer. Snow is going fast. After many hardships, and one mishap—a packhorse with his load fell into the river and drowned—the first pack train has arrived in the valley, coming over the Blue Mountains from the Umatilla Landing, bringing supplies to relieve the immediate needs of the people; also, bringing the cheering news that another pack train would soon arrive.

The manager told the people that if they would give him orders for what seed they needed, he would try to supply them in time for spring planting. This was a happy thought, and to many a great boon. But alas! Many had not the money to send for the seeds; their only hope was to get rations enough to last until the roads were open for travel, then leave the country.

The freighters would charge but little for their passage, and nothing if they were unable to pay, but they must provide their own rations for the trip. Many did leave that spring, saying that they hoped they would never see the valley again. Had they seen it sixty years later, as I have done, they would see the finest land the sun ever shone upon. I am glad I helped open it up!

One day while my brother-in-law Tom was making a garden, I gave him a bucketful of potato peelings, and told him to plant them. I had left the eyes pretty deep and had been saving them for that purpose. Sister Addie spoke up and said she had some, too. Frank had put the idea into our heads to save potato peels. I was peeling potatoes one day and throwing away the peels. Frank said, "Don't do that. It's a sin to throw away even one potato eye, because, if you plant it, it might raise half a dozen potatoes.

Tom planted the peels, and when he dug his potatoes that fall he sold one hundred fifty dollars worth— all grown from peels that ordinarily would have been thrown away.

I was anxious to get some chickens, but there were so few in the valley as to make them almost unobtainable. Our neighbor, Mr. Schooler, had brought back with him from Umatilla Landing a dozen hens, which he had bought at Walla Walla. His wife kept six for herself, and gave the other six to her mother-in-law and sister-in-law. By dint of much persuasion I finally induced her to let me have six chicks from the first brood. I paid her seventy-five cents each for them—a steep price for day-old chicks! I was very proud of my little brood, and I took especially good care of them.

Maybe you think pioneering and ranching in those days was easy on the womenfolk, with little housekeeping to do, and no club work or society affairs to attend. If you do, you have another think coming! All our cooking was done on the fireplace, and we were short of cooking utensils, besides. We had to get along with the few things we had brought in our wagons across the Plains the previous year. Cookstoves, such as we had back home, were not to be had, and cooking on the fire was very inconvenient. But withal, we kept our cabins neat and clean, and took pride in our personal appearance as we did back in our old homes, trying always to dress neatly and cleanly. The long trip across the Plains, dirty camping places, and the long stretches where we were unable to wash and keep ourselves clean, had not increased our liking for dirt; and here in our homes, we did love to make our surroundings clean and pleasant, that our husbands might enjoy them when they came in all tired out from their hard labors in the field, or from their long journeys to the mines, or after supplies.

The women were not alone in the use of primitive methods and tools, for the menfolk, too, had to do their work in an untoward way. Imagine the inconvenient manner of threshing their grain. After it was harvested in the most difficult yet the only way possible, it was taken to the threshing floor. For this purpose, a big, round space was selected, perhaps fifty feet in diameter. It was leveled and made as smooth as possible, first by scraping and dragging it until it was nearly level; then the surface was wet down and trampled to make it hard. This process was repeated time after time, after which it was allowed to dry and harden. A low pole fence was then built around it to keep the straw from spreading under the feet of the oxen.

A wagon load of grain was brought in and spread over the threshing floor; then four yoke of oxen were tied together and driven into the enclosure, and put to milling around. After the oxen had thoroughly tramped the straw, the men would stir it and shake it with their forks, and carefully throw it to one side to separate it from the grain. When the grain was tramped out as cleanly as possible, it was shoveled onto a canvas in the middle of the ring, and the floor was swept clean with brush and brooms made of willow twigs tied together. It required about half a day to thresh one filling of the enclosure.

After about two days of threshing the men stopped to try out the fanning mill [a machine for winnowing grain]. This, too, was slow, hard work, but the men took turns and kept it going rather steadily. When it was clean, the grain was sacked in bags imported from the Hawaiian Islands. The sacks were of good quality, but high in price.

It took nearly three weeks to finish threshing and sacking Jimmie's grain, then his crew helped Frank and Hugh.

Jimmie now began to haul his grain to market, a big job in itself. I do not recall how many bushels he had, but he told me he sold over eight hundred dollars worth. The government was keeping a full company of cavalry horses and several freight teams at the Fort, and this provided a good market for all the grain.

Next, Jimmie must dig and market his potatoes, after which he would be ready for their journey. He cleared about a thousand dollars by staying over that summer. My sister felt, however, that they must delay their journey somewhat, due to a coming event of importance in my household [the birth of Arabella's first child, Joseph Lee].

17
A STOVE, SOME NEW CHICKENS, AND ANNOYING CRITTERS

Ours were the only eggs in the country [at this time of year], and we could sell them at amazingly high prices; a tavern keeper paid Frank three dollars a dozen for the first that he took to town. The hotel keeper offered him two dollars a dozen for all he would bring until spring opened up and the laying season began.

ONLY THE MOST BASIC necessities were in early frontier homes. Comforts and refinements were neglected as there were few opportunities for making money, and hard, physical labor consumed everyone's time and energy.

On the frontier, change came in small increments. A new stove, a board floor to replace a dirt one, getting rid of bugs and mice, and the purchase of some good laying hens were big events in Boise in the late 1860s. Ambitious pioneer families grasped at any opportunity to raise needed cash.

Now, I must tell about my new cookstove, for, outside of marriages and births, I think it the most important happening of the time.

*An early photograph shows the interior
of a typical home in the Idaho Territory.*

Frank sold his oats to the government agent at the Fort for fifteen cents a pound. He brought back a No. 8 Charter Oak stove, made in St. Louis. If travel adds refinement and elegance, as some folks think, this stove could have passed muster in high society. It had traveled from the factory in St. Louis down the Mississippi on a river boat such as Mark Twain might have piloted; over the blue waters of the Gulf, crossing the procession of equinoxes, rounding the celebrated Cape Horn with its well-known stormy waters, on to the tranquil Pacific Ocean to Portland, Oregon; up the renowned Columbia River to Umatilla; thence by wagon freight across the picturesque Blue Mountains, finally reaching its destination, the Boise Valley, and coming as an honored guest to my house— although I soon put it to earning its keep, and more. It served the double purpose of cookstove and heater.

But after all, it was only a common stove, worth, where I came from, about twenty-five dollars. Frank paid one hundred twenty-five dollars for it. He also bought the lumber for covering the space where the chimney had stood, and enough to lay that part of the floor where we walked most in doing the housework.

Setting up the new stove was no small job, especially cutting a stove pipe hole through the roof, which was composed of mud, hay, sticks, and split poles all lapped together. Finally they decided to cut off the end of the roofing on one corner of the house, and after putting the pipe through, splice out the space with boards. This solved the problem and worked nicely.

When the owners of the pack train saw my new stove, they said it would suit them exactly if I would board them. They would sleep in the other house and make as little trouble as possible and would pay me well for their board for about six weeks.

I agreed and was now cooking for six men. But the cooking being plain, it was was not so hard to do. Dried apples were all the fruit we had, but there were plenty of vegetables in the cellar. Occasionally I made a squash or pumpkin pie, and every now and then a pudding. I had milk, but eggs were so high I could not afford to use them. However, I got along nicely with my boarding venture and the men all seemed satisfied.

By spring I had earned enough to pay for my stove.

Early that fall Frank had bought some chickens from Mr. Smith, the man who had brought the fine Dorking chickens across the Plains. He bought twenty-three pullets and one rooster, paying three dollars each for them. I had raised three pullets that summer by hand, so I had twenty-six hens to start the next season.

The men built a nice, warm chicken house of logs. A small opening was left for a window, over which they securely tacked a piece of white cloth. A wheat stack near the door gave the chickens a handy feeding place, and a little covered place in front afforded a dry scratching pen. We were greatly astonished when in mid-winter our pullets began to lay.

By the middle of March I had sold enough eggs to pay for my chickens, and now I began saving eggs for setting. When the snow went off, we opened up the hen house and let the chickens out during the day, but shut them up securely at night because of the cold and the varmints.

A hen I called Aunt Polly hatched my first brood. After her chicks were weaned, she again hatched another fine brood before the summer had ended.

Although I could get a dollar and a half a dozen for eggs, I would not sell any, for I was intent on raising as many chickens as I could that season, as I knew they would bring me a fine price on the market. I brought off sixty fine, little chicks my first hatch and put them into a box and brought them into the house to keep them from chilling.

Here they met a slight disaster, which caused me to lose some of them. First, they became overheated. To relieve them, I turned them out on the floor, and again they met with trouble. I left the room a short time, and when I returned I found the baby sitting in the midst of the chickens, holding one in each hand, squeezed to death! There he sat, putting the head of first one and then the other into his mouth.

Thereafter, I kept the baby away from my chicks, and I had such good luck with them that I soon had between three and four hundred. Nor did I neglect my garden. All our earlier garden vegetables came from it. It was a source of joy, and I loved it. I often took the baby with me, when the weather permitted, and sat him in a tub while I worked in the garden.

We bought our first hog late that spring, and how do you suppose hogs were brought into the valley? An enterprising resident of the valley went over into southern Oregon and bought a number of sows and stock hogs. He brought them by boat to Umatilla Landing and kept them there until the mountain roads were passable, then drove them afoot all that three hundred miles to the Boise Valley! We paid seventy-five dollars for a six-week-old sow. She soon brought us four little pigs, and from this one sow we got our start of hogs.

The previous spring, another man having an eye to the business possibilities of the country, and especially to its needs, launched another enterprise which might have made him some money, and also helped the community, had he been able to carry it through. He conceived the idea of bringing in a wagon load of cats, thinking to sell them at a good price. He went to Oregon and bought several crates of cats, but in crossing the Blue Mountains, he had the misfortune to overturn his wagon, breaking the crates and scattering the cats to the wilds. This was a sure-enough catastrophe. Mice were bad in the valley, and many of the settlers would have paid him as much as twenty-five dollars for a cat.

Mice were the worst nuisance we had to contend with. In winter they came in from the fields, and the houses were fairly filled with them. We had no means of protecting our supplies from them, and they occasioned us heavy losses. I have often wondered how we managed to save anything, having no tight boxes and canisters such as we have today.

Another very disagreeable nuisance which threatened to run us out of our homes was the low-lived bedbug. Where they came from was a puzzle to us for a long time. We were sure we had not brought them across the Plains. At first I felt too humiliated to mention them, and set myself resolutely to the task of hunting them down and eradicating them. In log cabins this was hard to do; there were so many places for them to crawl into.

One night a man from town came down to see Frank and told us: "Bedbugs are natural in this country. You can find them out here in the sagebrush sometimes, and they live in certain kinds of pine trees, around the limbs and knots. If you bring timber or lumber from the mountains, you are sure to get bedbugs. We old-timers always sleep out of doors in summer to avoid them."

We had another very annoying pest, which lasted only about six weeks in the year. It was a small, black gnat, and while it lasted, it was a terror to man and beast. It made its appearance about three o'clock each afternoon, and made life almost unbearable. It was impossible to work in the garden or do any other kind of outdoor labor, without first covering the face, neck, hands, and wrists.

And, of course, we had the omnipresent mosquito, and a most pestiferous pest he was, with his buzzing, singing, biting, blood-thirsty proclivities, making outdoor life most uncomfortable, and indoor life nearly as bad. Having no screens for the doors and windows, we had to fight mosquitoes as best we could. Smudging was our principal weapon, but the smoke was about as bad for us as it was for the mosquitoes, and when it was cleared away, in would come a swarm of the sleep-disturbing beasties, and the fight would be renewed. It continued until either we were too exhausted to care, or the mosquitoes were too full to bother.

18

THE COMMUNITY GROWS

With the organization of the county, Frank and Hugh were tendered political honors. Frank was appointed justice of the peace, and Hugh was appointed constable. Both took the matter as a joke, saying they were too busy to go to the county seat to qualify for office; so both offices and the emoluments thereof, were allowed to go by default.

THE VAST CHANGES in the West during the period that Arabella writes about were part of a great agricultural revolution that occurred at the same time as the industrial revolution took place in the East. These two revolutions are largely responsible for the successful settlement of the western part of the United States.

The process of Western settlement followed a pattern. The first people to live in the West were the Native Americans. Later, traders and trappers arrived, seeing an opportunity to make a living from the wildlife. They opened pathways for miners and cattle ranchers who came to the frontier in search of prosperity. The miners opened the Rocky Mountain region to settlement. Finally, small farmers who were hoping to better themselves followed the prospectors and cattle ranchers. But to succeed on their farms they needed the help of Eastern industry. Eastern factories produced strong steel plows, and new farm machines that were used to prepare the soil, plant the

An 1845 sketch of Oregon City,
the end of the Oregon Trail

seeds, and harvest the crops. Eastern factories built railroads to carry out the crops and take back materials for
building homes, coal to heat them, and furniture to make
them livable.

As soon as farm families had their applications for legal
title to the land approved by the government (state or ter-

ritorial), they built permanent homes to replace their log cabins, which they then used as sheds and storage bins. When more people arrived in a region, several families would join together to form a community, building sawmills and grain mills, setting up churches and schools, and starting businesses. The development of farm communities was the last stage in the settlement process in the West. As these communities matured, the frontier—with all its challenge and promise—passed into history.

Ours was a very isolated community during the long winters. When we spoke of anyone leaving, we said they were going "outside." We had but little reading matter; only the little weekly paper, and once in a while a copy of the Oregonian. A mail route had been started from Umatilla Landing, which gave us pretty good summer service, but in winter our mail was very uncertain. As an illustration of the dearth of our reading matter, the first winter after our marriage, I had come in possession of a copy of an English magazine, the contents of which were mainly fiction. I was always a lover of books, and this absorbing little fiction magazine was intensely interesting to me. It was all the fiction I had to read.

The Bible was the only book we had in the house for two or three years. I read it much that winter, and it had its influence on all of us.

The winter passed pleasantly, and spring came. The advent of the mill and of harvesting machinery gave everyone new impetus and new courage. I divided my chickens with my neighbors who had none, and Frank divided his young pigs among those who wished to get a start of hogs.

My hens, being well cared for, began laying early. At first, eggs were worth one dollar and twenty-five cents a dozen, but they soon dropped to one dollar, and later to seventy-five cents a dozen. Chickens were becoming more plentiful now. I would soon have four good milk cows, and hoped to make quite a lot of butter to sell. Butter was still one dollar a pound.

The men carried out their plans for a bigger and better grain crop, and soon it was looking so promising that they felt justified in buying a McCormick reaper. The reaper cost three hundred dollars at Umatilla Landing and had to be transported by freight team from that place. It cut and bunched the grain, but did not bind it. Five men followed after the machine, binding the grain, tying it into bundles with straw bands. With a large crew, and the machine, our harvesting was finished in much shorter time than it was the previous year.

That spring I helped Frank set out some fruit trees, mostly apples, which we got from a nursery in Walla Walla. This was the first orchard planted in Boise Valley, and the first home-grown apples ever seen in Boise City came from this orchard. We also had a fine lot of vegetables, such as melons, cucumbers, and tomatoes, although we made no special effort at gardening. I put up pickles and preserves and made tomato catsup for our winter use, but did no canning of fresh fruit and vegetables, for canning was not known to us then.

News reached us from Washington City to the effect that the lands in the valley would soon be surveyed. Idaho Territory had been organized. The people here were striving to get the seat of territorial government located at Boise City, and they were successful in the end, although the north country claimed Boise had stolen the capitol. All were glad, however, to see the matter settled, and glad to have their lands surveyed. [When a new territory was to be organized, one of the first steps was to survey the acreage. The

Bureau of Land Office in Washington handled this task. The bureau's surveyors also surveyed land claims of farmers. According to the formula set forth in the Homestead Act (1862), any adult citizen could claim 160 acres free, with the requirement that the claimant settle on the land and make certain improvements. To reduce land speculation and to encourage more settlers to move into a region, the government held to the 160-acre maximum (for a while, at least), and those holding more land than they were entitled to were required to sell the extra amount.]

The survey created a great many more homes for people; most of the settlers had taken up more land than they were entitled to. Frank and Hugh had previously bought an eighty-acre tract from a neighbor. This made their holdings larger than one person was entitled to, but not large enough for the two full components allowed each individual head of a family. Whereupon, Frank proposed to trade Hugh the home place, with its over-amount of land, for the Smith place, Hugh to pay the difference of sixteen hundred dollars. Hugh agreed to the offer, and he and Frank settled their land business before the survey came.

We also bought more cows. Our herd now consisted of fourteen head, all good milkers. We kept one hired man that year whose principal duty it was to help with the milking and to look after the cows. This year we sold five hundred dollars worth of fresh butter.

Dairy work was too much for my health, however, and Frank urged me to trade the cows for young stock, and build up a herd of range cattle. He had already quite a number of his own. To this I consented, reserving, however, six of my very best cows.

Frank worked energetically opening up his new farm. Considerable brush and willows had to be cleaned up, but the land was rich and productive.

Lumber was now becoming more plentiful in the

valley. The sawmill in the mountains had enlarged its capacity of sawing and shingle-making. Many of the settlers were replacing their log cabins with frame houses, not pretentious, but more comfortable than the old ones had been.

There were several children of school age in our community, but as yet we had no school building. The neighbors got together, selected a site on a cool, flowing stream, and planned a structure, having in mind not only the present, but the future needs of the growing community. There were shady nooks and a grassy playground for the children in play time, and the plot selected was a pretty one.

The community was liberal both with work and with money. A carpenter was hired to do the finishing, and to make the seats. The building was large enough not only for the school, but for the public gatherings, such as preaching, speaking, and social entertainment.

The first term, the attendance consisted of six boys only. But the next year there were four girls. One of our bachelor neighbors had married a widow with five children, four of them girls of school age. Soon another family came into the neighborhood, and two more school children added. This gave us a fair-sized rural school. But as yet, there had been no preaching or Sunday school in our community, the latter because of lack of children, and the former because of lack of a preacher. In another settlement down the canyon below us, there was both preaching and Sunday school conducted by a resident minister, the Elder Morrow. The emigrants who settled there had large families. Elder Morrow lived in the valley for many years, and so far as I know, kept up his ministerial work as long as he lived.

The next summer was a repetition of the preceding one, with plenty of hard work, but market condi-

The teacher and schoolchildren pose for a visiting photographer in front of their sod-covered frontier schoolhouse.

tions were not so good. The mines gradually played out, and did not furnish employment for nearly so many men. The government had greatly diminished its cavalry force at the Fort. All these things affected our market conditions.

A daily stage, operated by the Greathouse Brothers to the nearest railroad point, brought us in touch with the outside world. Hitherto, we had taken little interest in the papers; now we read about the great scandals and the grafting in the East. We learned of the strife and bickering; of the accusations and trials of men of prominence in the affairs of the nation; of the disgraceful conditions incident to the Reconstruction Period; of the graft in building the Union Pacific Railroad—that dark blot on the pages of the nation's history!

We learned, also, that there were some good, noble-hearted men of the North who were making brave efforts to secure mercy and justice for the fallen South.

But the evil effects of the War, and the inhuman treatment accorded the supporters of the Lost Cause [the Confederacy], proved a blessing to the West. It brought emigrants here by the thousands. Though many came from the North, the majority came from the war-ridden states. They met hardships and privations here, of course, but the later arrivals never felt the scarcity of food such as the earlier settlers had suffered.

On the sixth day of September, our third child was born. We named the baby Della, after no one in particular, but because we thought it a pretty name for her. I often laughingly said that I had named her after one of Brigham Young's wives, for that was where I had first heard the name. She was a very sprightly, active child, and at the age of ten months could climb the stake and rider fence to its top rail. Once I found her on the roof of the poultry house.

Late that fall we had the first preaching services in our neighborhood since the first summer we came. Then a Baptist missionary had preached three sermons for us. Now a preacher named Boli came over from the Walla Walla country on a missionary tour of his own undertaking. He was not sent from any organization, but was financing his own way. He was a Campbellite, a follower of Alexander Campbell who was a noted reformer of that day. As we usually entertained any stranger who came into the country, our place was recommended to him as one at which he might stop. He arrived on horseback, with a pair of saddle bags slung across the saddle. In them he carried a Bible, a dozen or so hymn books, and a change of linen. The latter was in need of washing, for he had been on the road a long time, having stopped and preached in the Payette Valley. But it was not linen, as I learned when I washed it. It was mostly woolen such as everybody usually wore for underwear. His wearing apparel was not of very good quality, and was much worn, and he had long, unkempt hair and beard. But in those days we never judged a man by his outward appearance. He told my husband his business, and asked for accommodations. Frank told him that we would be glad to keep him for a few days, and that we would be glad to have him preach at the schoolhouse.

This was on Friday, and as the preacher had had a long, hard ride that day, it was thought best to make the announcement that the preaching would be held Sunday morning and Sunday night.

Sunday morning found most of the people of the settlement at the schoolhouse. Those from a distance had come in lumber wagons or on horseback, and those nearer had come afoot. The back-woodsy look of the preacher may have occasioned some disappointment, but he was a vigorous speaker, and presented his doctrine with a firmness of conviction that aroused the interest of his congregation.

At this time, Jimmie and I were the only ones baptized. The preacher promised to come back later and hold another meeting about Christmas time, if he could cross the mountains.

At the appointed time he came back and we had a good meeting, with much interest, and splendid results. My sister and her husband had returned from

Oregon. While living in Oregon they had united with this church. Both were good singers and were a great help in our meetings. There were other good singers in attendance, and the song service was especially interesting. The meeting closed with ten candidates for baptism.

The weather had been very cold for some time and the ice on the river was frozen six or eight inches thick. A big hole had to be cut for the baptizing. The novelty of baptizing people through ice brought a large crowd. A newly-married couple living about ten miles down the river from us had come to visit some friends, and while here they had attended the meeting and were converted. The young woman had sent word to her mother that she was to be baptized and wished for a change of clothes for the occasion. The mother, being Methodist, did not believe in immersion, and could not see the need of being put under the ice. On the baptismal day she came up hurriedly and remonstrated with her daughter.

Pointing to the hole, she said: "I think it would take a brave soldier to go under that ice!"

"That's the kind we want, mother, the kind we need!" replied the daughter. The mother made no further objection, but helped prepare the daughter for the ordeal.

At the end of our two weeks' meeting we organized a little church of about thirty members.

19

ON TO TEXAS

*He little knew then how much cause for thank-
fulness that well-planned wagon was to be
before our journey ended!*

ON MAY 10, 1869, the Central Pacific and the Union Pacific
Railroads completed laying track from Omaha, Nebraska,
to Sacramento, California. As a result of the "wedding of the
rails," communication and transportation were changed
forever in the nation. Travelers could now make their way
from one coast of America to the other by rail.

The first transcontinental railroad was quickly followed
by four others. In order to earn profits, the railroads needed great numbers of paying customers. To get them, the
railroads advertised in the East and in Europe, offering
land at very low prices as an inducement to come West.
The people came by the millions. By 1900 the railroads
had brought about five million people to the West.

When the Civil War ended, the fast-growing cities of
the East provided a good market for beef, and the railroad
provided the means of delivering it. Thus, cattle-raising
very quickly turned into a big business. Enterprising small
farmers, such as Frank, saw in Texas longhorn cattle a
chance to make a great deal of money.

A ceremony at Promontory, Utah, marked the completion of the transcontinental railroad on May 10, 1869. There was some corruption associated with the construction of the railroads in the United States. The Union Pacific Railroad paid approximately $70 million to a dummy corporation, but the cost of building the railroad was actually only $50 million. Railroad executives pocketed the difference. Central Pacific Railroad executives benefited by a similar arrangement.

In Texas a thriving cattle kingdom grew and prospered. The main reason for this was that vast acres of grassland were free for the using. Because the cattle ranchers didn't have to pay any money to graze the cattle, their costs were low and their profits could be high. Unfortunately for the cattle ranchers, the free-grazing lands soon became overcrowded and the heyday of the cattle kingdom was short lived.

But even in the best of circumstances, cattle-raising was a tough business enterprise. Eventually the cattle ranchers had to buy and fence land, build barns, buy feed, and maintain their stock. All this required large amounts of capital. Many small ranchers could not compete with the wealthy business corporations that eventually took over the cattle country and had to sell out and leave.

The railroad was completed in 1869, and Frank decided to make a trip to his old home in Ohio. He promised to stop over at my old home in Missouri to see my father. My folks all wanted to see him, for they said my accounts of him were very favorable.

Frank wanted to take my father a present, and we had a hard time selecting something suitable. We finally decided to give him a meerschaum pipe. As a rule, meerschaum pipes were quite expensive, but we got a very good one for ten dollars. It was in a handsome case and looked very fine with its silver mountings and beautiful stem. It was pure white, but Frank explained to my father that the more he smoked it, the finer the color would get, and that the test of a good meerschaum was its ability to color well. We learned afterwards that father would never be able to smoke it. He said it was too nice to mess up with tobacco. He always kept it inside the case of an old clock on the mantlepiece, and he would take it out occasionally, wipe and polish it carefully, admire it awhile, then carefully put it back. When I visited him eight years later, he still had his pipe in the old clock and had never smoked it.

That winter we had hired a man to do the milking and to take care of the stock. A. E. Callaway had come down from the mines, and was staying with us, and he did most of the cooking, so I followed Frank's instructions to take a good rest. The children kept well, and baby Della, being healthy and contented, gave me little trouble. In my leisure time I pieced quilt tops.

Frank spent most of the following summer on the range with his cattle. He and Frank Robinson went farther out to a new range, which made long intervals between his visits home. We were always so glad to see him when he came home, and the baby was now so cute and sweet, that he tried to come home as often as possible. The hired men, being old-timers on the place, could go ahead with the farm work very well in his absence. In fact, the next year he rented his farm to them, and devoted all his time to his increasing herd and to preparing feed for their winter use.

Now that the road was finished, the Wells Fargo Company established an express service. This, in connection with the rail service, permitted us to get such articles as we needed. Our little families were growing fast, both in size and numbers. The children were subject to colds, croup, indigestion, eczema, etc., and we expected that whooping cough and measles would follow. In preparation for such exigencies, I bought a copy of *Dr. Gunn's Medical Adviser*, a very elaborate and comprehensive treatise on the cause and cure of diseases, especially those of children, and containing simple, household remedies for hundreds of ailments. It also contained a supplement, which gave instruc-

*An 1869 photograph shows the typical
stagecoach used by express companies
on the overland trails. Soldiers ride
atop the coach as guards.*

tions in obstetrics. This was a great help to me, not
only here, but later, for I have always lived on the
frontier where a doctor was not always to be had. All
we needed, in connection with Dr. Gunn's book, was to
know what the disease was; the remedy was easily
found. It served our purpose very well, and was the
only doctor we had in our family during the remainder
of the time we lived in Idaho.

That fall, some of the men of our neighborhood

conceived the idea of forming a company to buy a herd of those long-horned Texas cattle, which were then being brought in great droves to the Plains of the Northwest, replacing the herds of buffalo so ruthlessly exterminated during the building of the Union Pacific.

When the cattle arrived they were driven over to our place for branding, as we had good corrals for holding them. Never having seen Texas longhorns before, we considered them a queer lot of cattle. They had heavy heads, short bodies, and slender legs. In disposition they were not far removed from their wild state, their native home being the Mexican and Brazos plains. During the War many of the Southwestern homes had been broken up and destroyed by Indian depredations. The livestock, left to roam the wilds and subsist as best they could, had become as wild as they were in their primitive state. Handling these cattle was a fascinating but perilous undertaking.

No one understood branding cattle Texas style, so they built a chute in which to run the cattle for this operation, but it took much longer to brand them by this means, and three whole days were consumed at this work.

The night they finished branding and got the cattle started for the range, my fourth baby was born. Frank wanted to call her Arabella, for me, but I never liked the name. Then he suggested Isabelle, saying: "We can then call her Belle, as I have always called you." The little boys liked the name, too, so we named the baby Isabelle.

The men who had gone into the cattle deal with Frank either became disgusted with the looks of the cattle after comparing them with the home product, or the ridicule of the neighbors caused them to become dissatisfied, for first one and then another made

Frank an offer to sell out to him, and by spring he had the whole herd on his hands. He kept them two years, running them on the range with his other herd, and when he sold all his stock in 1872, their increase made him a handsome profit.

Frank really wanted to go to Texas to engage in cattle raising. Our present location was not an ideal place for that purpose. I was not in favor of the move; I had an intuitive feeling that it would not be best for us. Frank and I had several discussions on the subject, and finally, after an almost all night's talk, we came to a decision.

The morning after we had made our decision to go, Frank went down and told his friends (mainly Hugh Allen and his brother-in-law, Doc Callaway) we would go with them if they could wait for us to get ready. They said that they would not only wait for us, but would help us all they could in our preparations.

Now began some really busy, anxious, perplexing and strenuous days. We had considerable property to dispose of. We had two farms to be sold, a good-sized herd of range cattle, and a nice herd of dairy cattle. All of it being very desirable property, Frank sold it readily, but he had to allow time payment on some of it.

We planned to take two wagons on the trip, one with a four-horse team to carry the provisions, horse feed, and bulky articles, and one with two horses, for ourselves and some bedding. A man who had heard of our intended trip offered his services to Frank as driver and assistant, in return for his board and passage to Texas. Frank accepted this offer and gave him employment. He proved to be very faithful and efficient. The two little boys rode with him most of the time, and he treated them very kindly.

Frank had a hard time planning our wagon. He

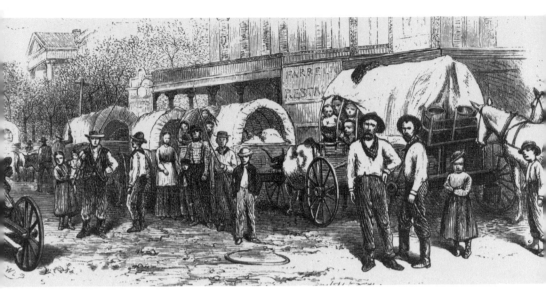

Moving on to Texas

wanted to make it as handy and as comfortable as possible. He had a carpenter make a double deck on the wagon, the upper part extending out four inches on each side, thus making the upper deck four feet wide, but allowing it to reach only to the wagon seat in front. This was the right length for a set of spiral bed springs. The springs had been sent to a merchant as a sample, and we had bought them some time before. They were the only springs, at that time, in the valley, and they had come from Ogden by ox team. The merchant sold them to us at cost, which was seven dollars.

The four-inch offset on each side of the wagon box was braced with four heavy iron braces on each side, which prevented any possibility of its breaking loose. A solid floor of smooth plank was put in the upper deck, and the springs placed on it. My new carpet

147

was placed on the springs, and on top of it was placed my feather bed—we had no mattresses in those days. It was a good bed, and it proved a blessing to me before the end of our trip.

Wagon sheets stretched on bows covered it and protected us from wind and rain, and we added an inner lining to the cover to break the intensity of the sun's rays. In this lining I made pockets to hold my thimbles and needles, and thread, and other articles. When I got tired of holding the baby, or when she wanted to sleep, I could turn and lay her back on the bed without getting up from my seat. Little three-year-old Della had a nice place there for sleep or play. The wagon sheet was fastened so securely at the sides and end that there was no danger of her falling out. At the back part of the wagon cover we had an apron, which we could remove for letting in fresh air.

After it became generally known that we were planning to go, two other families said they would like to join us. One of them was Mr. More, the man who had erected the first flour mill in the valley. He had sold the mill and wished to find a new location. The other was Mr. Greathouse, the man who operated the stage line from Boise to the railroad in Salt Lake City. He also had recently disposed of his holdings, and intended to leave the valley. He and Frank were old friends. We were glad to have such good friends go with us.

In all, the train consisted of ten wagons and eight families—forty-three people, counting children. Though small, it made an imposing appearance, everything being new and well-furnished.

We had a secret, which at the time none dared to mention. Now, after the lapse of about sixty years, I am free to tell it. I am the only survivor among the grownups of that train, although several of the children are yet living. Our secret was that the train carried a considerable amount of money, so much that it would have made a fine haul, indeed, for some of the bandit bands that infested the country. Luckily for us, however, we never happened onto any of them. In our small train of ten wagons I imagine we carried with us a far greater amount of money than we did on that former journey in 1864, in which more than a hundred wagons crossed the Plains.

On the morning of April 15, 1872, we started on our journey to seek new homes in a new country.

20
EPILOGUE

THE JOURNEY TO TEXAS turned out to be arduous, as Arabella had feared it would, and was a portent of the next ten hard years in that unforgiving land. The wagon train traveled slowly first toward Ogden, Utah, then to Salt Lake City, and Denver, down the Big Thompson Valley, where the settlers intended to turn south to go on the Wichita Cattle Trail. But instead of following this path, the travelers changed direction and turned east, then south through the plains of western Kansas, adding 500 miles to their journey. Their general direction was southeasterly toward Indian territory.

At Coffeyville, Kansas, they crossed the Arkansas River, and entered Oklahoma. When they crossed the Red River, they arrived in Texas, ending their long journey on Bear Creek.

From the very beginning, Texas tormented the family and nearly broke their spirit. In this land barren of people and crops, the Fultons and their friends endured grinding poverty, near starvation, and serious illnesses; they suf-

*Traces of the Oregon Trail are visible today
near U.S. Highway 30, in Umatilla County,
Oregon. While sagebrush covers some of
the wagon tracks, others can still be seen.*

fered through actual Indian attacks, worried about rumors of others, and barely survived the long, harsh winters.

The farm lay about 60 miles from Dallas, in Wise County. The nearest town was Decatur, located some ten miles away. Although Arabella valiantly tried to like her Texas home, her memoir is filled with dispirited accounts of aggressive black snakes eating all her chicken eggs, and the annoying presence of rattlesnakes, tarantulas, centipedes, seed ticks, and chiggers (harvest mites). Worst of all were the harrowing "northers"—violent storms that arrived without warning, day or night, often causing widespread destruction.

Yet, they did survive and their tiny community grew larger, but was not especially prosperous. The settlers organized and started a school and a church, and the community's social life expanded. Arabella's memoir describes how everyone suffered through several years of poor crops, unbearably freezing winters, and a scarcity of bread and meat. Some of her friends became so discouraged that they packed up and left the area. Always, though, new emigrants arrived to take their places, most coming from the Southern states, seeking to begin new lives after their defeat in the Civil War.

Eventually Frank, too, gave up on Texas and he and Arabella decided to move back to the Northwest. They had had enough of malaria, the children's endless misery with contagious "sore eyes," boils, broken bones, and snakebites. Then, too, there were heavy stock losses caused by cattle and horse thieves who roamed through Texas at that time. Frank finally agreed that his wife had been right in her intuitive fear that the move to Texas would prove disastrous.

On April 15, 1883, Arabella, Frank, and the children, including a sickly new baby, joined a wagon train leaving for the Northwest Territory. This train consisted of 88 people in 17 families, 24 wagons, and 115 horses. At first they followed the cattle trail to Fort Dodge, then took the Chisholm

Trail, so rutted from the many wagons that traveled it over the years that the ride was terribly uncomfortable all the way to Kansas.

The trails to Denver and Wyoming were also deeply rutted from emigrants' wagons, and the Fultons jolted and swayed and made slow progress all the way to South Pass and into Idaho and Oregon. After four and half months, they reached the territory of Washington.

The Fultons bought land in the Kittitas Valley, which lay twelve miles northeast of Ellensburg, Washington, on Coleman Creek. It was valley land, rich and good, and on this land they built a fine stock farm, raised a great flock of chickens, tilled an abundant kitchen garden, and raised a prize dairy herd. With their usual hard work they prospered, and within a few years were doing well enough to build a lovely home for themselves and their children, who now numbered ten.

Arabella Clemens Fulton spent the remainder of her life in this home place. In December 1930, at age 86, she completed her memoir saying, "the joy of living it all over again as I write it, is a recompense for my labor, and to you, my children, I leave this record."

Arabella Clemens Fulton died July 29, 1934, at the home of her daughter, Della, near the old Fulton place outside of Ellensburg, Washington. She is buried in the Ellensburg cemetery, beside her loved ones.

FOR FURTHER READING

Andrist, Ralph K., and editors of American Heritage. *The Calilfornia Gold Rush.* New York: American Heritage Publishing Co., 1961.

———. *To the Pacific with Lewis and Clark.* New York: American Heritage Publishing Co., 1967.

Blumberg, Rhoda. *The Great American Gold Rush.* New York: Bradbury Press, 1989.

Montgomery, Elizabeth Rider. *When Pioneers Pushed West to Oregon.* Champaign, Ill.: Garrard Publishing Co., 1970.

Parkman, Francis. *The Oregon Trail.* New York: Airmont Publishing Co., 1964.

Place, Marian T. *Westward on the Oregon Trail.* New York: American Heritage Publishing Co., 1962.

Ross, Nancy Wilson. *Heroines of the Early West.* New York: Random House, 1960.

Rounds, Glen. *The Prairie Schooners.* New York: Holiday House, 1968.

Smith, C. Carter. *Exploring the Frontier: A Sourcebook*

on the American West. Brookfield, Conn.: Millbrook Press, 1992.

Steck-Vaughn Library. *Voices from Our Nation.* Austin, Tex.: 1991.

Stewart, George R. *The Pioneers Go West.* New York: Random House, 1954; reprinted 1987.

INDEX

Note: Page numbers in italics indicate illustrations.

156